Praise for *The Hidden History of the Supreme Court and the Betrayal of America*

"Hartmann looks at the Supreme Court today as a tool of the right and their corporate interests. He reminds us that the Declaration of Independence promises 'life, liberty, and the pursuit of happiness,' not 'property,' and urges 'we the people' to lawfully subject SCOTUS to democratic governance."

—**Harvey J. Kaye, Professor of Democracy and Justice Studies, University of Wisconsin–Green Bay, and author of *Thomas Paine and the Promise of America***

"Thom Hartmann has created an elegant historical road map that reveals how one of the most influential judicial bodies on the planet evolved into such a powerful and mysterious entity."

—**Mike Papantonio, host of *America's Lawyer***

"Thom Hartmann provides a clear-eyed view of the right-wing assault on the courts—and a principled vision for restoring justice for the many, not just the few."

—**Lee Fang, investigative journalist**

"Thom Hartmann gives fascinating play-by-play coverage of the federal judiciary's fall from the 'most harmless branch' of government to a clear and present danger to liberty and democracy. Do you want to understand how the plutocrats are trying to gavel down on We the People? Read. This. Book."

—**Alan Grayson, former member of Congress**

T0205153

"A brilliant, highly readable account of the least-understood democratic branch of our government, its growing power, and its hijacking by the right, this book is essential reading for anyone who's concerned with the future of our democracy and the fate of our world."

—Richard Eskow, writer, journalist, consultant, and broadcaster

"Hartmann has the amazing ability to bring important history to life. His new book is a must-read for people of all political persuasions to understand the history of the Court and its political impact. It is an eye-opener on the betrayal of America and what it means for our future."

—Bob Ney, Political Analyst, Talk Media News, and former member of Congress

"In a provocative and easy read, Hartmann warns we have ceded enormous political and economic power to the wealthy classes, despite our founding fathers' intention to place more corrective power in the hands of the electorate."

—Bill Luther, former member of Congress

"Hartmann once again goes deep to understand the origin of the crisis in the Supreme Court, which didn't stem from Trump alone. To understand the power of the Court, its dangerously dysfunctional state, and what you can do, read this book."

—Dahr Jamail, author of *The End of Ice*

THE
HIDDEN HISTORY *of*
THE
SUPREME
COURT
AND THE BETRAYAL OF
AMERICA

THOM HARTMANN

BK
Berrett–Koehler Publishers, Inc.

Berrett-Koehler Publishers, Inc.
1333 Broadway, Suite 1000
Oakland, CA 94612-1921
Tel: (510) 817-2277
Fax: (510) 817-2278
www.bkconnection.com

ORDERING INFORMATION
Quantity sales. Special discounts are available on quantity purchases by corporations, associations, and others. For details, contact the "Special Sales Department" at the Berrett-Koehler address above.
Individual sales. Berrett-Koehler publications are available through most bookstores. They can also be ordered directly from Berrett-Koehler: Tel: (800) 929-2929; Fax: (802) 864-7626; www.bkconnection.com.
Orders for college textbook / course adoption use. Please contact Berrett-Koehler: Tel: (800) 929-2929; Fax: (802) 864-7626.

Distributed to the U.S. trade and internationally by Penguin Random House Publisher Services.

Berrett-Koehler and the BK logo are registered trademarks of Berrett-Koehler Publishers, Inc.

Printed in the United States of America

Berrett-Koehler books are printed on long-lasting acid-free paper. When it is available, we choose paper that has been manufactured by environmentally responsible processes. These may include using trees grown in sustainable forests, incorporating recycled paper, minimizing chlorine in bleaching, or recycling the energy produced at the paper mill.

Library of Congress Cataloging-in-Publication Data
Names: Hartmann, Thom, 1951– author.
Title: The hidden history of the Supreme Court and the betrayal of America / Thom Hartmann.
Description: Oakland, CA : Berrett-Koehler Publishers, 2019. | Series: The Thom Hartmann hidden history series ; 2
Identifiers: LCCN 2019009594 | ISBN 9781523085941 (paperback)
Subjects: LCSH: United States. Supreme Court--History. | Political questions and judicial power--United States.--History. | Constitutional history--United States. | BISAC: HISTORY / United States / General. | LAW / Constitutional. | POLITICAL SCIENCE / Government / General.
Classification: LCC KF8748 .H367 2019 | DDC 347.73/2609--dc23
LC record available at https://lccn.loc.gov/2019009594

First Edition
27 26 25 24   10 9 8 7 6 5 4 3

Book production: Linda Jupiter Productions; *Cover design:* Wes Youssi, M.80 Design; *Edit:* Elissa Rabellino; *Proofread:* Mary Kanable; *Index:* Paula C. Durbin-Westby

CONTENTS

A Rebellion against the Monarchy

The candid citizen must confess that if the policy of the government, upon vital questions, affecting the whole people, is to be irrevocably fixed by decisions of the Supreme Court, the instant they are made, [then] in ordinary litigation between parties in personal actions the people will have ceased to be their own rulers, having, to that extent, practically resigned their government into the hands of that eminent [Supreme Court] tribunal.

—Abraham Lincoln, from his first inaugural speech, explaining why he refused to recognize the Supreme Court's *Dred Scott* decision

From the time Americans wake up in the morning, throughout their days (work or play), right through a full night's sleep, everything they do, touch, ingest, breathe, and use has been touched in one way or another by the Supreme Court.

Food, drugs, transportation, clothes, furniture, roadways, water, septic, electricity—everything in modern life is regulated in some way, either in manufacture, distribution, sale, or use, and those regulations are allowed or disallowed, ultimately, by the US Supreme Court.

At home and in the workplace, Americans' lives are regulated by the Supreme Court: whether there can be a minimum wage or unemployment insurance; how much power employers can have over labor unions and employees; whether consumers can sue when harmed by products or corporate actions; and how far police and other agencies can go in prosecuting (sometimes persecuting) individuals or entire groups of people.

The Court determines and defines the limits of your right to protest and your right to a free press. It has final say in everything from taxation to regulation, from public space to private space, from contraception to marriage. Both directly and indirectly, the Court determines how wealth can be earned, accumulated, and disposed of; it decides how far the rich can go in exploiting the poor and working people, and whether working people can fight back.

Meanwhile, America has ended up—mostly since around 1980—with one of the most corrupted political systems in the developed world, with billionaires and big corporations literally writing legislation to benefit themselves, from the federal to state to local levels.

As Tim Wu[1] wrote for the *New York Times* in March 2019, "About 75 percent of Americans favor higher taxes for the ultrawealthy.[2] The idea of a federal law that would guarantee paid maternity leave attracts 67 percent support.[3] Eighty-three percent favor strong net neutrality rules for broadband,[4] and more than 60 percent want stronger privacy laws.[5] Seventy-one percent think we should be able to buy drugs imported from Canada,[6] and 92 percent want Medicare to negotiate for lower drug prices."

Yet Congress as a whole has not even once seriously considered any of these things in decades. The reason, quite simply, is literally billions of dollars of politically poisonous cash flowing from corporations and ideologically motivated billionaires into the bloodstream of our body politic.

And it wasn't Congress or any president in history who changed laws to make this possible; it was the Supreme Court.

Right now, and throughout much of US history, the ideological makeup of the US Supreme Court has had little resemblance to the political makeup of our nation.

In 2019, for instance, solid majorities of Americans supported a woman's right to access abortion and birth control, voting rights, a national health care system, well-funded public schools and free education through college, higher taxes on corporations to pay for infrastructure and an expanded social safety net, and regulation of corporate behavior from pollution to banking.

These are issues that enjoy *majority* support from working Americans and American communities, but not from corporate America or America's billionaires.

As this book shows in parts 1 and 2, the Court has historically almost always sided with the wealthy, the powerful, and the corporate against the poor, the weak, and the individual.

In many cases, these decisions have struck down laws passed by Congress and signed by the president, a process called *judicial review*.

This book answers the core questions about the Supreme Court's decisive role in determining the fate of the planet: Why did the framers create the Supreme Court? What is judicial review—and how does it make the Supreme Court what Thomas Jefferson, post-1803, called a "despotic" branch? How does the history of the US Constitution explain the Court's frequent decisions in favor of the wealthy and corporations? When *has* the Court sided with popular opinion—and how have people successfully challenged the Court in the past? How did a 20th-century coalition of businesses and billionaires seize control of the American government, including the Supreme Court, and why is this now a planetary crisis?

Most important, what can Americans do about all of this?

In the Beginning . . .

There were those among the founders and framers of the Constitution who didn't mean for the Court to have this much power—Thomas Jefferson among them. Part 1 of this book dives into the philosophies that guided the men who drafted the Constitution. It also shows how in 1803, the Supreme Court set itself above Congress and the president with the power to review, strike down, or rewrite laws based on its own lone interpretation of the Constitution.

Importantly, the framers of the Constitution gave no consideration to "the rights of nature" or even of the environment, other than its sheer productive potential to enhance the wealth of the nation.

Instead of the environment, when the Constitution was written in the summer and fall of 1787, the new thing in political circles was the idea of property rights for commoners, which had only clearly been articulated outside of the realm of royal prerogatives during the previous few centuries.

John Locke wrote in his 1689 *Two Treatises of Government* that the main purpose of government was to make sure that "no-one may take away or damage anything that contributes to the preservation of someone else's life, liberty, health, limb, or goods."[7] He was speaking directly to the new ability of some commoners to actually claim title to things, including their own bodies.

After 1,000-plus years of either the monarch or the church (or both) wielding absolute rule and absolute ownership of *everything*, Locke was pushing a radical and revolutionary idea.

In his chapter titled "Political or Civil Society," Locke noted that both the laws of *nature* and the laws of a *civilized society* would give the right of "life, liberty and possessions" to every man.[8]

If that language seems familiar, it's because Locke is the man whom Thomas Jefferson plagiarized, or was inspired by, when he wrote in the Declaration of Independence that the purpose of our newly formed government was to provide for "life, liberty and the pursuit of happiness" because we had the right, simply as humans, to "assume among the powers of the earth, the separate and equal station to which the Laws of Nature and of Nature's God entitle [us]."

A Suicide Pact

By the time Jefferson was writing, a mere century after Locke, the right of "commoners" (at least white male ones; women and people of color were still excluded) to own private property was well established and well recognized, so Jefferson didn't see the need to restate it. Instead, he replaced Locke's repeated and varied mentions of different types of property with "happiness." It was the first time that word ever appeared in the founding documents of any nation.

Thus, the newest revolution in human rights in 1787, brought to North America by Enlightenment philosophers like Jefferson, was the idea of nonwealthy "commoners" having individual *property rights*—the right to private ownership of things: from the food a person grew; to the land on which they lived; to exerting agency over their own lives, workplaces, and bodies.

The concept of property rights was becoming a core Western philosophy in the 17th and 18th centuries, and one of the core functions of our 18th-century Constitution was to protect, regulate, and provide a mechanism to adjudicate those property rights. Without the Stuart monarchies' losing their absolute power over property rights in the English Civil War of 1642–51 and the Glorious Revolution of 1688, the Industrial Revolution may never have happened.[9] This shift of property rights, including land rights, from the Crown to the *people* (at least the white male people) created the legal and political floor for the thinking that led to the American Revolution.

But in 1787, the framers weren't concerned about running out of arable land, clean water, and clean air. And they never imagined a time when several versions of that day's East India Company would rise up on these shores and take over our political system to their own advantage and to the disadvantage of democracy itself. They were far more worried about how to create a republic in which the government would both protect a person's right to own property and facilitate his (consideration of women was excluded) enjoyment of it (hence, "the pursuit of happiness").

Today, all of that is at risk.

The world is facing a climate crisis that could very well end civilization as it's currently known, and perhaps could even lead to the death of every animal on earth larger than a dog (including humans), as has happened five times in our geologic past.[10] Fossil-fuel interests are steering the planet toward those very undesirable outcomes at light-warp speed. If something isn't done about the climate/carbon crisis, people reading this book today might be living in the last generation to experience a stable atmosphere, and thus a stable form of governance, for any foreseeable future.

The Supreme Court has seized the power to decide what is "constitutional," and it uses that power to strike down or rewrite laws that have been passed by Congress and signed by the president. But because our Constitution doesn't mention the rights of nature (or even the environment), the Earth's biosphere is getting short shrift in our legal system—no matter how many laws Congress passes to protect the environment.

Thus, the judiciary has turned our Constitution in the direction of, as Thomas Jefferson feared, becoming a suicide pact.

Corporate America Seizes the Court

In many ways, the looming crisis is one created by the Supreme Court itself.

No legislature, governor, or president has ever suggested that corporations should be considered "persons" for the purpose of constitutional protections, particularly under the 14th Amendment's equal-protection rights.

No federal or state legislature, no president, and no state governor has ever, in more than 240 years, suggested that billionaires and corporations have a First Amendment "right" to unlimited political bribery. Congress has instead criminalized such behavior repeatedly.

Both doctrines, *corporate personhood* and *money as speech*, were simply invented by corporate-friendly Supreme Court rulings (in the 1819–86 era for corporate personhood, and in the 1976–2013 era for money as speech). Their combined effect has been to hijack America's democratic experiment, concentrating power into the boardrooms of faceless corporations and the summer homes of reclusive billionaires.

As President Jimmy Carter told me some years ago, America is no longer a functioning democratic republic; we've devolved into an oligarchy.[11] Most of this crisis is the direct result of the Supreme Court's use of judicial review.

Political power is now defined by wealth. That means that virtually unlimited political power has been concentrated into the hands of the richest industry in the world, the fossil-fuel industry—the very same industry that is endangering every aspect of our modern world with its reckless pursuit of ever-increasing profits.

The corruption that brought us to this point started with a 1971 memo, in which Republican activist Lewis Powell suggested to the US Chamber of Commerce (and the corporations and multimillionaires associated with it) that they should actively involve themselves in politics. They did, and were so successful that Republican presidents now look to petro-billionaire-funded organizations to select judicial nominees for the federal bench, including the Supreme Court.

How did America's great democratic experiment end in a functional oligarchy? And how can we change course in time to address the planetary crisis of climate change?

Part 2 details when and how the Court has ruled in favor of the country's elite, and how presidents and the people themselves have occasionally gone to war with the Court—and won.

With those histories in mind, part 3 of this book presents constitutionally available solutions for Americans to rein in the Supreme Court and claw back our democracy from the hands of billionaires and corporations—including one particularly startling "emergency" solution suggested by John Roberts when he worked for Reagan.

The Hidden History of Judicial Review

To understand the Supreme Court, one must understand the zeitgeist of the Founding Fathers' generation and the philosophical history that led the founders and framers to create the Court itself.

Part 1 of this book looks at the founders' intents and concerns—and how quickly the Court seized the power of judicial review to become a nearly despotic branch of government. The conclusion of part 1 explores how one man sparked a right-wing movement to seize control of the American government—including the outsized power of the Supreme Court.

The Founders' Vision

*The accumulation of all powers, legislative, executive, and
judiciary, in the same hands, whether of one, a few, or many,
and whether hereditary, self-appointed, or elective, may justly be
pronounced the very definition of tyranny.*

—James Madison

In May 1787, a group of men in Philadelphia began to gather
to debate and discuss what would become the template for the
new United States of America: a new constitution. The youngest was New Jersey's 26-year-old Jonathan Dayton (although
James Madison was in his 30s, as were several other delegates),
and the oldest was Pennsylvania's Ben Franklin, who at 81 was
so infirm that he had to be carried to and from the meetings.

Five men who were not in the room influenced the convention tremendously. Thomas Jefferson was stationed in Paris as
the US envoy to France; John Adams was in London as our
envoy to the UK. But even more important, Thomas Hobbes
was 108 years dead, John Locke had been dead for 83 years,
and Baron de Montesquieu had been dead for 32 years.

Thomas Hobbes tutored King Charles II and wrote *Levia-
than*, which triggered the earliest stages of the Enlightenment,
and also the big split away from monarchy and toward liberal
democracy.

Hobbes's ideas, with their faith in hierarchy and patriarchy,
also formed a basis for today's conservative movement. He
believed that the essential nature of humans was evil (because,
the Bible tells us, we're all "born of woman") and that man's
"original state" was a life of continual warfare and fear: "During
the time men live without a common power to keep them all

in awe . . . [they have no] arts; no letters; no society; and which is worst of all, continual fear, and danger of violent death: and the life of man, solitary, poor, nasty, brutish and short."

The only escape from our brutish and fearful existence in the state of nature, according to Hobbes, was under the iron-fisted institutions of church or state.

This is still the primary conservative narrative: without the restraining force of church or state, human life will devolve into chaos. A strong father figure, the story goes, is necessary, both in the form of leaders and rulers, and in the form of a tutelary (to use Alexis de Tocqueville's word) state.

This view also led to the formation of the Supreme Court.

The Glue That Binds Us Together

Two generations after Hobbes, in the 1600s, King James II's tutor, John Locke, saw things differently. He saw balance and democracy in nature and believed that humans could live in the then-modern world without submitting to some "dear leader." Instead, he wrote that humans could live "in society." He described it as the collection, both biological and voluntary, of people living in proximity and united for a common goal with a shared philosophy of social organization.

Locke's *Two Treatises of Government* tore the "divine right" argument[1] for ruling to pieces in 1690, making Locke famous and vaulting him to the front of the philosophers who were arguing for something more egalitarian to replace royalty.

His *Second Treatise* laid out the basis of democracy, as he saw it, and set the stage for today's modern liberal democracies and the overall arc of the US Constitution.

Locke argued against the king's supreme power over person and property, declaring, "Man being born, as has been proved, with a title to perfect freedom . . . hath by nature a power . . . to preserve his property, that is, his life, liberty and estate, against the injuries and attempts of other men."

Nearly a century later, Locke's language informed Thomas Jefferson's drafting of the Declaration of Independence. Because Locke conceived of law as being above any individual (such as a king), his argument called for a *court system*.

Another towering figure who influenced the creation of the Supreme Court was Charles-Louis de Secondat, aka the Baron de La Brède et de Montesquieu. Long gone but still well remembered, he was simply referred to by the founders and framers as Montesquieu.

Montesquieu argued in his 1748 *The Spirit of Laws* that egalitarian, democratic societies could work,[2] and Jefferson wholly embraced Montesquieu's ideas about the separation of powers within a government.

One could argue that Montesquieu was the godfather of the Supreme Court.

A Bold Experiment

Delegates also considered the form of democratic government held by the Iroquois Confederacy, as evinced by Ben Franklin, who wrote to his partner in the publishing business in New York, James Parker:

> *It would be a very strange Thing, if six Nations of*
> *Ignorant Savages should be capable of forming a Scheme*

for such an Union, and be able to execute it in such a Manner, as that it has subsisted Ages, and appears indissoluble; and yet that a like Union should be impracticable for ten or a Dozen English Colonies, to whom it is more necessary, and must be more advantageous; and who cannot be supposed to want an equal Understanding of their Interests.[3]

The Iroquois had a court system that, in some ways, also inspired our Supreme Court.

Jefferson knew the Indians of Virginia well; as a young boy and early teen, he had traveled from remote tribe to tribe with his father, who spoke several of their languages, while his father was mapping the state. In his 1785 *Notes on Virginia*, Jefferson vigorously defended the Iroquois, and the Native Americans in general, against those Hobbesians who argued that they were uncivilized brutes.

Jefferson dismissed the racist rhetoric of the day, explaining, "In short, this [uncivilized] picture is not applicable to any nation of Indians I have ever known or heard of in North America." Favoring history over racist myths, Franklin and Jefferson each looked to aspects of the Iroquois Confederacy to inform our own Constitution.

At the time, most of the contemporary "civilized" world still operated with the assumption of the divine rights of kings: the idea of private ownership of property as a normal thing for white working men was only about a century old (and wouldn't appear for women until the 20th century).

After the failure of the Articles of Confederation to hold the nation together, the framers knew that there were lessons to be learned from scholarly Western sources, such as the ancient Greeks and Romans, but also from more novel sources, including the Iroquois elders they invited in for the opening days of the Convention.

These men were embarking on a bold experiment.

Debating the Supreme Court

From the founding of our republic in 1789 until 1803, the Supreme Court was only the final court of appeals. After all, the buck had to stop somewhere.

In 1788, when James Madison and Alexander Hamilton published a long series of newspaper articles promoting to the American people the idea that they should ratify the Constitution (which happened in 1789), Hamilton took on the job of selling Article III, which created the court system, including the Supreme Court.

In that sales pitch, Hamilton, on May 28, 1788, wrote in a newspaper article we today call the *Federalist*, no. 78, that the courts, including the Supreme Court, were the weakest of the three branches created by the Constitution.

"[T]he judiciary is beyond comparison the weakest of the three departments of power," he wrote, adding in the same sentence that "it can never attack with success either of the other two [branches]."

He even footnoted that sentence with a quote from the famous French judge Montesquieu, who had first clearly articulated the idea of a separation of powers between governmental branches as a check and balance. Hamilton's footnote read, "The celebrated Montesquieu, speaking of them, says: 'Of the three powers above mentioned, the judiciary is next to nothing.'"

He explained why the Court's judges had lifetime appointments and the judiciary had its own section of the Constitution, writing in the *Federalist*, no. 78, "[F]rom the natural feebleness of the judiciary, it is in continual jeopardy of being overpowered, awed, or influenced by its co-ordinate branches."

The lifetime appointments and Montesquieu's "separation of powers" would insulate the Court from being "overpowered, awed, or influenced" by the president or Congress.

But some Americans (and many of the newspapers of the day) weren't convinced; the idea of lifetime appointments and being a branch of government independent from the other two sounded too much like the European monarchies that the colonists had just fought a revolutionary war against.

"What would prevent the Supreme Court from rising up and taking over the country?" they asked. "You're concentrating too much power in one branch!" others essentially said.

So, a month later, in June 1788, Hamilton published what is now known as the *Federalist*, no. 81, answering directly their objections, again arguing that the Supreme Court couldn't make laws and couldn't strike down laws.

First, he cited (rather accurately) the objections to a Supreme Court in the Constitution that he was pushing, noting that they were concerned that judges—dangerously!—might interpret the Constitution in a way of their own personal choosing.

The arguments, or rather suggestions, upon which this charge is founded, are to this effect: "The authority of the proposed Supreme Court of the United States, which is to be a separate and independent body, will be superior to that of the legislature. The power of construing the laws according to the SPIRIT of the Constitution, will enable that court to mould them into whatever shape it may think proper; especially as its decisions will not be in any manner subject to the revision or correction of the legislative body. This is as unprecedented as it is dangerous [emphasis Hamilton's]."

Having set up the objections/concerns, he then answered those doubters in the next paragraph.

In the first place, there is not a syllable in the plan under consideration which DIRECTLY empowers the national courts to construe the laws according to the spirit of the Constitution, or which gives them any greater latitude in this respect than may be claimed by the courts of every State.

He also pointed out, in the next paragraph, that even if the Court were to rule on the meaning of a poorly written law (or even corruptly distort a law's meaning) in deciding a case, the legislature could simply write a new law clarifying what they meant and the new law would apply for the future: "A legislature, without exceeding its province . . . may prescribe a new rule for future cases."

Where Does the New Buck Stop?

Still, people were concerned that the Court would have too much power. What if they started striking down laws passed by Congress and signed by the president, both elected by We the People?

Hamilton's answer in the *Federalist*, no. 81, was that the Constitution itself prevented such an abuse of power, because the Supreme Court was explicitly subordinate to Congress.

We have seen that the original jurisdiction of the Supreme Court would be confined to two classes of causes, and those of a nature rarely to occur [arguments between the states, and treaties with other nations]. In all other cases of federal cognizance, the original jurisdiction would appertain to the inferior tribunals; and the Supreme Court would have nothing more than an appellate jurisdiction, "with such EXCEPTIONS and under such REGULATIONS as the Congress shall make."

If that wasn't clear enough, in the next sentence Hamilton essentially repeated himself.

To avoid all inconveniencies, it will be safest to declare generally, that the Supreme Court shall possess appellate jurisdiction both as to law and FACT, and that this jurisdiction shall be subject to such EXCEPTIONS and regulations as the national legislature may prescribe. This will enable the [rest of the] government to modify it in such a manner as will best answer the ends of public justice and security.

Yet, in the *Federalist*, no. 78, Hamilton had essentially endorsed judicial review.

> *The interpretation of the laws is the proper and peculiar province of the courts.*
>
> *A constitution is, in fact, and must be regarded by the judges, as a fundamental law. It therefore belongs to them to ascertain its meaning, as well as the meaning of any particular act proceeding from the legislative body. If there should happen to be an irreconcilable variance between the two, that which has the superior obligation and validity ought, of course, to be preferred; or, in other words, the Constitution ought to be preferred to the statute, the intention of the people to the intention of their agents.*

Having basically said that the Supreme Court actually has more power than the legislative or executive branches (contradicting his earlier "most harmless branch" claim), Hamilton tried to walk it back with the slight that "the people" is where the real power is, not the legislature, and the Court is ultimately representing "the people" who collectively elected the men in the states who ratified the Constitution. He noted in the *Federalist*, no. 78:

> *Nor does this conclusion by any means suppose a superiority of the judicial to the legislative power. It only supposes that the power of the people is superior to both; and that where the will of the legislature, declared in its statutes, stands in opposition to that of the people, declared in the Constitution, the judges ought to be governed by the latter rather than the former.*

Hamilton had pulled off a remarkable feat: he gave each side what they wanted, while trying to minimize either's effect on the other. And right up until 1803, nobody was really sure how much power the Supreme Court had.

Meanwhile, the rest of the framers (and their peers among the founding generation) were all over the map on what they thought the judiciary powers outlined in the Constitution meant, and on whether they wanted the courts to have such vast and largely unchecked and undemocratic power as represented by judicial review.

The Power Grab

June 28, 2012, was a day of high drama in Washington, DC. With more sun than clouds, it was a bright and hot day, over 90 degrees, as people lined up outside the Supreme Court to hear the fate of President Barack Obama's signature legislative effort, the Affordable Care Act. Across the nation, people with preexisting conditions and low-income working people hoping for free access to Medicaid held their collective breaths.

The Supreme Court didn't disappoint. The decision, with all four of the liberal justices joined by Chief Justice John Roberts, ruled that the Act itself *was*, in fact, constitutional, with a couple of caveats.

The first was that they justified their decision by determining that the penalty that uninsured people must pay was actually a tax, and therefore the Act was within the taxing powers of Congress and thus constitutional.

The second was that the Medicaid expansion, which would have covered every low-income working person in the country (almost half of all workers), couldn't be forced on the states but only adopted with the consent of the states, one at a time.

Nobody doubted that the Supreme Court had the power to strike down the law in its entirety, or to uphold it entirely, or even to rewrite parts of it or parse it into pieces, which is what happened.

Similarly, nobody questioned why the most powerful branch of government, the one with the final say over pretty much everything, was also the one that never had to submit itself to we the people in an election or suffer any other form of accountability.

Although President Obama—a constitutional law professor earlier in his life—had already signaled that he'd go along with whatever the Court ruled, two prior presidents, Jackson and Lincoln, had refused to comply with orders of the Court. They'd held the opinion that each branch of government was able to determine its own perspective on the constitutionality of laws, given that each branch was supposed to be "coequal" and the members of each took an oath to uphold the Constitution.

In the *Federalist*, no. 49, for example, the father of the Constitution, James Madison, wrote, "The several departments being perfectly co-ordinate by the terms of their common commission, neither of them, it is evident, can pretend to an exclusive or superior right of settling the boundaries between their respective powers."

Challenging the power of the Supreme Court has largely been the province of the hard right in the United States, starting with the Court's flip to go along with Roosevelt's New Deal in 1937, and flaming into full flower in response to *Brown v. Board of Education* and *Roe v. Wade*.

But with a right-wing takeover of the Court in the late 20th and early 21st centuries, under dubious circumstances (detailed later in this book), America is moving back to the perspective on the Court that was widely held between 1933 and 1937—that it was out of control and may need to be tamed.

The Constitution, in Article VI, Section 2, established *constitutional supremacy*, saying, "This Constitution, and the Laws of the United States . . . shall be the supreme Law of the Land." It thus, unambiguously, gave the Supreme Court the power to overturn state laws and state courts. As Chief Justice John Marshall (1801–35) wrote in the *McCulloch v. Maryland* decision (1819), "The [federal] government of the Union, though limited in its power, is supreme within its sphere of action."

This establishment of federal supremacy and judicial review over state laws wasn't particularly controversial.

But when the Supreme Court, in 1803, ruled that it had the power to overturn acts of the federal Congress, signed into law by the president, all hell broke loose, at least in the mind of President Jefferson, and the echoes continue to this day.

They provide us with context, arguments, and ways to remedy some of the recent years' most egregious excesses of the Supreme Court.

Whoever Controls the Law Controls the Country

Article III of the Constitution creates the federal judiciary and lays out how it operates and what its powers are. Article III, Section 2, deals specifically with the Supreme Court and explicitly puts the Court—the Supreme Court—*under* the "regulation" of Congress. Congress is also given the power by the Constitution to write laws that specify "exceptions" when the Supreme Court can't second-guess them.

Article III, Section 2, reads simply:

> *In all Cases affecting Ambassadors, other public Ministers and Consuls, and those in which a State shall be Party, the supreme Court shall have original Jurisdiction. In all the other Cases before mentioned, the supreme Court shall have appellate Jurisdiction, both as to Law and Fact, with such Exceptions, and under such Regulations as the Congress shall make [emphasis mine].*

In other words, the framers empowered the Supreme Court for two main reasons: first, to hear disputes between the United States and foreign countries, and between the individual states; second, to be the final court of appeals.

But nowhere does the Constitution explicitly say that the Supreme Court has the power to decide what is or is not "constitutional," or to strike down (or make or modify) laws or policies for the United States.

So where did the concept of judicial review come from? How did the Supreme Court (and even lower courts) get the power to review laws to decide what laws are constitutional and what laws are to be thrown out?

It started with a battle between Thomas Jefferson and John Adams, which was carried out in proxy by the war between Adams's Federalists (today we'd call them conservatives) and Jefferson's Anti-Federalists (today we'd call them liberals). Between the time when Jefferson won the election of November 1800 and the time he took office in March 1801, President Adams flooded the federal bench with brand-new positions and brand-new hyper-Federalist judges in an aggressive court-packing scheme.

Jefferson thought he found a loophole in the Judiciary Act of 1789: if a new judge had not received his judicial appointment papers physically and in person, he couldn't take a seat on the bench. When Jefferson entered the White House, he discovered that Adams had been so hasty in his court-packing plan that there was still a large pile of appointments waiting to be delivered.

Secretary of State James Madison had the legal authority and responsibility to deliver the papers, and Jefferson instead ordered Madison to throw them away, thereby depriving the Adams-appointed judges of their seats on the new Adams-created courts.

One of the appointed judges, William Marbury, sued Madison for not delivering his papers, and the case went straight to the Supreme Court.

In the resulting 1803 case of *Marbury v. Madison*, the Supreme Court found that the judiciary has the power to strike down any law passed by Congress and signed by the president.

Chief Justice John Marshall, appointed by Adams, was a vigorous Federalist, a distant relative of Jefferson, and a political archenemy of Jefferson. He wrote in his decision, "It is emphatically the duty of the Judicial Department to say what the law is."

Marshall's ruling declared unilaterally that the Court's powers included interpreting the meaning of the Constitution and applying that interpretation to federal legislation.

After empowering the Court with judicial review, Marshall ruled in Jefferson and Madison's favor. Marshall first ruled that Madison had broken the law by refusing to deliver the papers. But the Court then struck down the portion of the Judiciary Act that required the papers to be delivered, leaving Marbury out in the cold.

It horrified Jefferson that Marshall had so intruded into the legislature's domain by striking down a law that Congress had passed and President George Washington had signed. Jefferson immediately wrote to John Adams's wife, Abigail, a confidante:

> The opinion which gives to the judges the right to decide what laws are constitutional, and what not, not only for themselves in their own sphere of action, but for the legislature and executive also, in their spheres, would make the judiciary a despotic branch.

Those who control the law, Jefferson was saying, control the nation. In a single stroke, Marshall had put himself and his fellow justices *above* both Congress and the president.

Jefferson later protested to his old friend, Virginia Supreme Court Justice Spencer Roane,

> If this [Marbury] opinion be sound, then indeed is our constitution a complete felo de se [suicide pact]. . . .

The Constitution, on this hypothesis, is a mere thing of wax in the hands of the judiciary.[4]

Jefferson: "The People Themselves"

Supporters of judicial review argue, "If we don't have the Supreme Court deciding which laws are constitutional and which are not, then who should?"

To that, Jefferson had a simple answer: "The people themselves" through their elected officials in Congress. Congress, after all, has the power of both *Exception* and *Regulation* of the Supreme Court in Article III, Section 2, of the Constitution.

In 1823, Jefferson explained to his friend the Marquis de Lafayette how the Court had usurped power directly from the people: "The ultimate arbiter is the people of the Union, assembled by their deputies in convention, at the call of Congress, or of two-thirds of the States. Let them decide to which they mean to give an authority claimed by two of their organs [branches of government]."

Jefferson was arguing that because the Constitution represents the will of the people, constitutional questions are supposed to be answered by the people's representatives during constitutional conventions, as laid out in the Constitution itself.

In Jefferson's mind, that was how a democratic republic worked. With Marshall's invocation of judicial review, Jefferson thought America had become a constitutional monarchy, with the Supreme Court wearing the crown.

Jefferson's rage seemed to restrain the Court.

From 1803 until long after his death, the Court did not exercise judicial review in any way that alerted the public, did not strike down any significant laws, and did not create any national doctrines (although it did often refer to the Constitution).[5]

It wasn't until long after Jefferson and Marshall were both dead that Chief Justice Roger Taney sought to use the Court's power to settle the long-standing national debate about slavery in the United States. Taney's 1856 decision in *Dred Scott v. Sandford*, that African Americans *everywhere* in the United States were merely property, reflected his own slave-owning upbringing, and his constitutional interpretation reflected that of the Southern slave-owning framers.

Abraham Lincoln, an increasingly famous Republican political operative at the time, decried Taney thoroughly for it in a now-famous speech on June 26, 1857.[6]

Taney's 1856 interpretation didn't solve anything, and South Carolina seceded from the United States just four years later, kicking off the Civil War.

Even before Lincoln became president, he refused to recognize the judicial review component of *Dred Scott*, and he declared in 1857, "We think the *Dred Scott* decision is erroneous."

Who Decides What the Constitution Means?

Norman Solomon et al. compiled from Reuters and publicly available polling sources in October 2018 the following:

- 76 percent of the US public supports higher taxes on the wealthy.[7]

- 70 percent of the US public supports Medicare for all.[8]

- 59 percent of the US public supports an $15 minimum wage.[9]

- 60 percent of the US public supports expanded tuition-free college.[10]

- 69 percent of the US public supports abortion rights.[11]

- 94 percent of the US public supports an Equal Rights Amendment.[12]

- 59 percent of the US public supports stricter environmental regulation.[13]

The five Republican-appointed justices on the Court as of this writing are hostile to each of these positions. The views of these members of the Court are stuck in 1930, while the American people have fully moved into the 21st century. This contradiction is, on its own, nothing less than a constitutional crisis.

The Court is, in many ways, forcing America to live under an 18th-century form of government, recognizing property rights for humans but not recognizing human rights more broadly.

For example, while we no longer countenance slavery,[14] we have private prisons that the Court has said can be run, essentially, like plantations. While we say we've ended voting discrimination, people of color cannot vote and fully participate in society in parts of America[15] because the Supreme Court gutted the Voting Rights Act in 2013's *Shelby County v. Holder* decision.[16] While America has come a long way on workers' rights, the Court has severely restricted employees' right to sue when discriminated against or harmed in the workplace and their right to form a union.[17]

Americans also realize that the framers couldn't have imagined many of today's issues and may not have been sympathetic, for example, to same-sex marriage, abortion rights, or universal health care and Social Security (although some, like Thomas Paine, advocated for the latter two).

Today, another collision confronts America as more and more progressive politicians attain national office and push for more and more progressive policies.

Will the current Supreme Court—dominated by *originalist* Republican-appointed judges—allow for progressive legislation to move America forward? Or will the Court restrain Congress, the president, and the American people by handing down arcane interpretations of the Constitution to prevent popular policies?

The story of a 1971 memo by Lewis Powell sheds some light on what Americans are up against.

The Powell Memo and the Court

The modern-day corruption of the Court has its roots deep in a memo prepared in 1971 by Lewis Powell. The memo outlined how very wealthy donors and big business could take over both US public opinion and, eventually, the US government itself. And just months after Powell delivered it to his friend and a director of the US Chamber of Commerce,

Eugene Sydnor Jr., President Nixon appointed Powell to the Supreme Court.

Ten months after the Senate confirmed Powell to the Court, the public learned about the Powell Memo (the actual written document had the word "Confidential" at the top—a sign that Powell himself hoped it would never see daylight outside of the rarefied circles of his rich friends).[18] By then, it had found its way to the desks of CEOs all across the nation and was already being turned into real right-wing actions, policies, and institutions.

The FBI didn't find the memo during its investigation into Powell during his Senate confirmation; investigative journalist Jack Anderson did, though, and he exposed it in a September 28, 1972, column titled, "Powell's Lesson to Business Aired."[19]

Noting when the memo was discovered, Anderson wrote, "Senators . . . never got a chance to ask Powell whether he might use his position on the Supreme Court to put his ideas into practice and to influence the court in behalf of business interests."

A section of Powell's memo, "Neglected Opportunity in the Courts," detailed the strategy that has largely been followed to this day.[20] Noting the Court's power, Powell wrote,

> *Under our constitutional system, especially with an activist-minded Supreme Court, the judiciary may be the most important instrument for social, economic and political change. . . . This is a vast area of opportunity for the Chamber, if it is willing to undertake the role of spokesman for American business and if, in turn, business is willing to provide the funds.*

Laying out specifics, Powell added,

*The Chamber would need a highly competent staff of
lawyers. In special situations it should be authorized to
engage, to appear as counsel amicus in the Supreme Court,
lawyers of national standing and reputation. The greatest
care should be exercised in selecting the cases in which to
participate, or the suits to institute. But the opportunity
merits the necessary effort.*

The wealthy heeded Powell's message, fundamentally trans-forming America.

In 1971, only 175 companies had registered lobbyists.
By 1982, there were nearly 2,500. Today there are tens of
thousands.

The American Legislative Exchange Council (ALEC) was
founded in 1973. So, too, was the Heritage Foundation. And
in 1977, the CATO Institute was founded, first as the Charles
Koch Foundation, and then renamed a few years later as
CATO.

To Powell, nothing was more important than freeing the
very rich and their corporations from the shackles of regu-lation that prevented them from outright owning politicians
and the political process.

In the 1976 *Buckley v. Valeo* decision, the Court ruled that
political money is speech, implying that those who have more
money have more free speech in our political system. That
same year, in *United States v. Martin Linen Supply Co.*, the Court
gave corporations Fifth Amendment protections against dou-ble jeopardy. And in *Virginia State Board of Pharmacy v. Vir-ginia Citizens Consumer Council*, the Supreme Court ruled that
advertising is a protected form of free speech.[21]

In 1978's *First National Bank of Boston v. Bellotti*, Lewis Powell himself authored the decision that overturned state restrictions on corporate political spending, saying such restrictions violated the First Amendment.

Justices White, Brennan, and Marshall dissented: "The special status of corporations has placed them in a position to control vast amounts of economic power which may, if not regulated, dominate not only our economy but the very heart of our democracy, the electoral process."

But they had lost the vote, and political corruption of everything from local elections to the Supreme Court itself was now virtually assured.

Then came the Federalist Society, which built a nationwide network of jurists, attorneys, legal scholars, and politicians to indoctrinate a new generation's legal system with Powell's mantra: Corporate personhood is real, money is speech, democracy is mob rule, and organized money should always have privilege over organized people. The Federalist Society was founded in 1982 with millions of dollars in funding from the Koch-connected Bradley Foundation.[22]

Madison's concept that "government should have a common interest with the people" had finally been put down like a rabid dog.

Partisan Politics in "Original Intent"

The immediate goal of the Powell Memo was to have large corporations and billionaires fund an ideological machine that could capture the US government. The short-term goal was to put a halt to the wave of environmental and consumer protections championed by Rachel Carson and Ralph Nader (named in the document). The system that Powell advocated instead was, essentially, an oligarchy.

Once Powell joined the Supreme Court in 1972, he dutifully championed the "right" of oligarchs to own politicians in the 1976 *Buckley v. Valeo* and 1978 *First National Bank of Boston v. Bellotti* decisions.

Ever since those successes, Republican politicians have worked hard to get more Lewis Powell types on the Supreme Court: men who would always defer to corporate power and great wealth, and who would always work to turn America into even more of an oligarchy.

The first step in this process was to change the language that judges used to describe their pro-billionaire and pro-corporate judicial philosophy.

In 1938, Justice Hugo Black pointed out that the 14th Amendment—part of the post–Civil War trilogy that was supposed to free the slaves and grant equal protection under the law to all *people*—was mostly being used at the Supreme Court to argue for *corporate rights*:

> *Of the cases in this court in which the Fourteenth Amendment was applied during its first fifty years after its adoption, less than one half of one percent invoked it in protection of the Negro race, and more than fifty percent asked that its benefits be extended to corporations.*[23]

Public trust waned in the Court over the first three decades of the 20th century because of these pro-corporate rulings.

If the Court was to regain the public's trust while still helping the rich and powerful, it needed new language to justify its oligarchic behavior.

Enter *originalism* and *textualism*.

Originalism Is Joined by Textualism

Robert Bork's 1987 nomination hearing brought originalism and textualism into the American mainstream.[24] By the time President Reagan nominated Bork, Bork had already given business a big win by crafting an argument in 1966 that the Court used to decide 1977's *Continental Television v. GTE Sylvania*, rendering America's antitrust laws toothless.[25]

That year, the Court adopted Bork's view that antitrust laws were not in place to protect small competitors, to protect communities or legislatures from corruption, or to maintain a vibrant marketplace where entrepreneurs have a chance. Instead, Bork said, the *only* thing that courts should look at when enforcing antitrust law is whether consumers are seeing higher prices than they should.

No legislature ever came up with this idea, and it's certainly not what any of our antitrust laws say. But Bork had been pushing the idea in conservative circles for over a decade, and the Court loved it. Their adoption of the Bork Doctrine in 1977 began the process that gave us cheap Chinese junk and low prices on everything from toys to burgers, but also wiped out literally millions of small and local businesses.

Bork's doctrine, and its enthusiastic embrace by the Reagan administration after the Supreme Court made it the law of the land in *GTE Sylvania*, is the main reason why every American city today looks pretty much like every other one, with the same low-cost fast-food joints, chain hotels, and Walmarts.

More famously, Bork argued that the framers of the Constitution would never have countenanced gay people getting married or women getting abortions. Nine years after the Senate turned him down, he was still at it, arguing in a 1996 article:

> *The Court moved a long way toward making homosexual conduct a constitutional right, adopted the radical feminist view that men and women are essentially identical, continued to view the First Amendment as a protection of self-gratification rather than of the free articulation of ideas, and overturned two hundred years of history to hold that political patronage is unconstitutional.*[26]

Appealing to the founders' 18th-century sense of straight white male power is at the core of what is now called originalist theory. Bork's big mistake was going into specifics.

Originalists John Roberts, Neil Gorsuch, Brett Kavanaugh, Clarence Thomas, Samuel Alito, and Antonin Scalia refused, during their Senate confirmation hearings, to give specifics when asked about such topics. Instead, they said that their job was to view the meaning of the Constitution through the eyes of the men who wrote it—full stop.

Likewise, textualist justices pretend to divine the meaning of words in the Constitution by reading dictionaries from the 1700s. As Scalia told Fox News' Chris Wallace, "Originalism is sort of a subspecies of textualism. Textualism means you are governed by the text. That's the only thing that is relevant to your decision, not whether the outcome is desirable, not whether legislative history says this or that."[27]

But there's no *single* meaning to terms that appear in the Constitution like *general welfare, right, unreasonable, probable cause, equal protection, cruel and unusual, excessive,* and *due process.* Since the first decade after the Constitution was ratified, different courts and different states have interpreted each of these phrases differently.

And originalists say that we can't listen to the "plain words" of founders like Madison, Jefferson, or George Mason, because each of them served as an elected politician at one time or another, and therefore they must have had "partisan agendas." Originalists prefer to dive deep into arcane books to support their theories. Sometimes they find support for their ideas in texts that were almost certainly unknown to any of the framers of the Constitution.

To find an "individual right to bear arms" during the founding era, Scalia dug up a 1789 Pennsylvania Anti-Federalist tract published to argue against that state ratifying the Constitution.

Titled *Dissent of the Minority of the Pennsylvania Convention,* it had virtually nothing to do with guns and nothing whatsoever to do with the men who wrote the Constitution (it actually defied them). But Scalia wrote that the dissenting minority in Pennsylvania "unequivocally referred to individual rights," and from there he concluded that the same meaning must exist in the Second Amendment in the 2008 case *District of Columbia v. Heller.*[28]

Justice John Paul Stevens called Scalia out in his dissent: "The Court's atomistic, word-by-word approach to construing the [Second] Amendment calls to mind the parable of the six blind men and the elephant."

But it didn't matter how badly—or obviously—Scalia had twisted both law and history; all that mattered was that five votes on the Court supported protecting the "right" to own guns from state, local, or national regulation. And those justices sold the idea to Americans by pretending to cite the founders and framers.

One True Spokesman

The founders and framers were generally interested in a constitution that would reflect the changing needs and mores of the times. After all, they'd fought a revolutionary war against a nation that had been ruled by an inherited aristocracy for centuries. As times and opinions changed, British colonists like Washington and Jefferson decided to change their very own form of government—and they were willing to die to make it happen.

Thomas Jefferson was one of the most articulate and thoughtful of the founders to address this issue, and he put forth a biting critique of the constitutional philosophy now known as originalism.

Eight years after he left the White House, Jefferson received a pamphlet and a letter from Samuel Kercheval, a Virginia innkeeper and the author of *History of the Valley of Virginia*.[29] Kercheval wondered about the possibility of reforming the political system in Virginia with an eye possibly to a larger, federal reform. In both cases, Kercheval's main concern was with the difference in representation of the people in the House of Representatives and the Senate.

Jefferson replied at length in a July 12, 1816, letter. When he discovered that Kercheval had shared the letter with others, Jefferson asked Kercheval to retrieve and destroy any copies of the letter because he didn't want to get dragged back into Virginia politics. The letter still survives, though, and it provides some unfiltered insights into Jefferson's—and many of the founders'—thoughts on the Constitution and the American form of government.[30] He wrote:

> *Some men look at constitutions with sanctimonious reverence, and deem them like the ark of the covenant, too sacred to be touched. They ascribe to the men of the preceding age a wisdom more than human, and suppose what they did to be beyond amendment.*
>
> *As [the human mind] becomes more developed, more enlightened, as new discoveries are made, new truths disclosed, and manners and opinions change with the change of circumstances, institutions must advance also, and keep pace with the times. We might as well require a man to wear still the coat which fitted him when a boy, as civilized society to remain ever under the regimen of their barbarous ancestors. . . .*
>
> *But the dead have no rights. . . . This corporeal globe, and everything upon it, belong to its present corporeal inhabitants, during their generation. They alone have a right to direct what is the concern of themselves alone, and to declare the law of that direction; and this declaration can only be made by their majority.*

Jefferson was clear in his horror at what might happen if the Constitution could not grow with the times:

> *If this avenue be shut to the call of sufferance, it will make itself heard through that of force, and we shall go on, as other nations are doing, in the endless circle of oppression, rebellion, reformation; and oppression, rebellion, reformation, again; and so on forever.*

One great irony here is that Jefferson started the first free public college (the University of Virginia) and wanted every ward in every county to have a free public primary school. He argued strongly that democracy wasn't possible unless the populace was educated and informed.

Yet, if every school in America had vigorously taught civics and included the above letter from Jefferson—which has been publicly available since at least the 1850s—then when the conservatives of the 1980s first trotted out the entire idea of originalism, they would have been laughed out of the room.

As Republican President Ulysses Grant wrote in his *Personal Memoirs*, "It is preposterous to suppose that the people of one generation can lay down the best and only rules of government for all who are to come after them, and under unforeseen contingencies."[31]

Most preposterous of all? The idea that five men on the US Supreme Court, trained and promoted through their lifetimes by the billionaire-funded Federalist Society, can magically read the minds of the long-dead framers of the Constitution and dictate to Americans that they are the framers' only true spokesmen.

Clear Preferences versus Ambiguities

Since the founding of the republic, scholars and lawyers have debated what the framers of the Constitution meant by ambiguous principles like *general welfare* and *cruel and unusual*. But there is little ambiguity in the structural parts of the Constitution.

A few examples: each state will have two senators, and the Senate will vote to ratify treaties and execute impeachments; candidates for president must be 35 years old (on the other hand, *natural born* has had different popular interpretations over the years, and it's never been adjudicated by the Court).

While these structural items are amenable to change with changing times, the *principles* are where changing times produce the greatest swings in interpretation.

At the creation of the Constitution, for example, there was no broadly understood concept of the environment or how it related to government. Yet today, not only can a changing environment disrupt a democratic form of government, but it could even lead to the extinction of humanity itself.

The word *principle* appears more than 1,500 times in the collected writings of Thomas Jefferson. Principle, he suggested, was at the core of everything a government should be or do. He wrote in 1816: "Only lay down true principles, and adhere to them inflexibly. Do not be frightened into their surrender by the alarms of the timid, or the croakings of wealth against the ascendency of the people."[32]

Since President Franklin Roosevelt proposed and signed the law creating Social Security, conservatives have argued

that the framers never meant for the principle of "general welfare" to include policies like Social Security.

Conservative billionaires and corporations tried for years
to control the law legislatively. But starting with the Powell
Memo, cultural and religious conservatives joined up with the
billionaire and business class to recapture functional control
of the Supreme Court as a much easier way to seize power
than messy elections.

We the people can elect members of Congress and presidents all day long, but as long as the Court holds the power to
strike down laws (or even replace laws with new doctrines, as
they did in *Dred Scott*, *Plessy*, *Roe*, *Heller*, *Citizens United*, and
others), the Supreme Court (and its inferior federal courts)
has final say over the present and future of America.

And while ideologues control the Court and dance to the
tunes of those with great wealth and corporate power, the
Court will likely continue to deny Americans the policies, no
matter how popular, that could improve their lot in life and
American democracy.

The Corruption of the Court Itself

In the *Federalist*, no. 52, James Madison noted,

> *As it is essential to liberty that the government in general
> should have a common interest with the people, so it is
> particularly essential that the branch of it under consider-
> ation should have an immediate dependence on, and an
> intimate sympathy with, the people.*

The word *dependence* was no mistake; the concept was widely understood in the interdependent times of the Revolutionary era. Women, children, and enslaved people were dependent on white men; white men were dependent on wealthy white men who owned their land or employed them; and even the "independent" homesteader was dependent on his neighbors for everything from barn building to trading tools and foodstuffs and helping in times of sickness or injury.

In the *Federalist*, no. 57, Madison expanded on the idea that "the rich" shouldn't end up being the ones running our government:

> *Who are to be the electors of the federal representatives? Not the rich, more than the poor; not the learned, more than the ignorant; not the haughty heirs of distinguished names, more than the humble sons of obscurity and unpropitious fortune.... No qualification of wealth, of birth, of religious faith, or of civil profession is permitted to fetter the judgement or disappoint the inclination of the people.*[33]

Sadly, Madison's vision has largely died. Today, both Congress and the presidency have been corrupted by great wealth, and the corruption has become so systemic that it has spread to the Supreme Court.

In 2014, Matthew Gilens and Benjamin I. Page published an extraordinary study that found that the political goals of Americans in the bottom 90 percent of income are, essentially, ignored by the US Congress, the Supreme Court, and the presidency.[34] The political goals of the top 10 percent, however, predictably become law.

As Gilens and Page explained in the *Washington Post*,

> *Strong support among the affluent is associated with about a 25 point greater probability of a policy being adopted . . . while strong support among the middle class is actually associated with a small decline in the likelihood that a policy will be adopted. . . . In other words, strong support among high-income Americans roughly doubles the probability that a policy will be adopted; strong support among the middle class has essentially no effect.*[35]

Basically, the most elite and wealthy Americans simply get the legislation and Supreme Court decisions they want, when they want it. For average Americans, though, the probability of their wants and needs being addressed legislatively is even less likely than random chance.

When looking at a few generations' worth of Supreme Court decisions, we see a similar pattern.

Many Americans know this is true. And fossil-fuel billionaires have successfully exploited this frustration in the recent past. In 2010, average Americans, angry about the corruption of Congress and the White House, signed up to join the Koch-backed Tea Party—without realizing where it came from—and they marched in the streets to demand that their access to affordable health insurance be taken away.

It was one of the most spectacular head-fakes in the history of American politics.[36]

In 2016, Donald Trump likewise exploited Americans' frustration about political corruption, famously using the slogan that he'd "drain the swamp" to gin up his supporters before appointing numerous lobbyists to run agencies like the Interior Department and the EPA, among others.

Fossil Fuels Seize the Court

Less well known is how the very same billionaires and the fossil-fuel industry (among others) have corrupted the Supreme Court and large swaths of the federal and state judiciaries.

In November 2017, the *Washington Post* ran a story with the headline "Federalist Society, White House cooperation on judges paying benefits."[37] The article, authored by Robert Barnes, outlined how a private organization originally funded by fossil-fuel and beer billionaires (among others) was acting as the sole filter for determining who would be presented to the Trump administration for consideration as nominees for federal or Supreme Court positions.

Earlier in the year, there had been some urgency around the issue, as Republican Senate Majority Leader Mitch McConnell did something never before even seriously considered in the United States: he refused to allow President Obama's nominee for the Supreme Court, Merrick Garland, to have even a single hearing.

The clock ran out on the Obama presidency. Incoming President Donald Trump brought forth Neil Gorsuch. (Neil is the son of Anne Gorsuch, who resigned in disgrace from Reagan's EPA after dismantling dozens of environmental protections that polluters hated.)

As then, White House Counsel Don McGahn explained to Barnes, Senate Republicans even blocked President Obama from appointing judges to lower courts. That meant that "'the number of vacancies that was on the table when the president was sworn in was unprecedented,' McGahn said. He praised 'the courage that Mitch McConnell showed to make that happen.'"

Then, on January 28, 2018, the lead of a *Washington Post* story announced: "The Koch network is expanding its portfolio into the judicial branch."[38]

The article explained that the fossil-fuel billionaire Koch brothers (and their billionaire buddies) were going to fund an effort to get hard-right judges onto both the Supreme Court and other federal and state courts. Their colleague in this would be the hard-right, partially Koch-funded Federalist Society.

The day before, Kathryn Watson reported for CBS News, "The network backed by Charles and David Koch realizes 2018 will be a challenging environment—and they're going 'all in' to defend their policy priorities and candidates who support them, to the likely tune of roughly $400 million."[39]

If the Republicans could hold the Senate in the 2018 elections, they could continue to pack the federal courts and the Supreme Court with billionaire- and corporate-friendly justices. (On just one day, February 8, 2019, Republicans in the Senate pushed through fully 44 judges onto the federal bench, after preventing[40] President Obama's nominations consistently through his last two years in office.[41] As the headline read on an August 2017 *Daily Signal* story by Fred Lucas,[42] "Trump Appoints More Judges in 200 Days Than Obama, Bush, Clinton."

The luxurious hunting retreat where Antonin Scalia died was owned and run by John Poindexter, who owns a company with over 4,000 employees and whose company had had a case before the Supreme Court. As Eric Lipton reported in the *New York Times* in 2016,

> *Though that trip has brought new attention to the justice's penchant for travel, it was in addition to the 258 subsidized trips that he took from 2004 to 2014. Justice Scalia went on at least 23 privately funded trips in 2014 alone to places like Hawaii, Ireland and Switzerland, giving speeches, participating in moot court events or teaching classes. A few weeks before his death, he was in Singapore and Hong Kong.*[43]

Justice Thomas took only 86 subsidized trips in the previous 11 years, but his wife worked for years for the Koch-funded Heritage Foundation and brought home a very ample salary for her efforts.

Were Scalia or Thomas on any other federal bench, they would have been subject to the federal code of judicial ethics ("Code of Conduct for United States Judges"), and that code of ethics would have likely forced them to recuse themselves in the *Citizens United* ruling, among other consequential cases during their tenures. The Supreme Court, however, has chosen to ignore federal ethics rules.

From 2013 until her death in 2018, U.S. Representative Louise Slaughter annually proposed a federal law creating a Supreme Court code of ethics (after all, the Constitution allows Congress to "regulate" the Supreme Court). Slaughter told NBC in 2017, "We want the same code of ethics for the Supreme Court that we require for all federal judges. Just as simple as that."[44]

Republicans have consistently prevented the code of ethics from becoming law.

But even a code of ethics won't prevent billionaire political donors from helping decide who gets put on the Court itself. That would require a major rewrite of the rules of money in politics, something that Congress has done repeatedly, and the Supreme Court has repeatedly struck down those rules or weakened them to the point of inconsequentiality.

Right-Wing Takeover and Corporate Handouts

Mitch McConnell, Senate majority leader at the time of this writing, knows that the Supreme Court and US judiciary have more lasting impacts on our democracy than does Congress.

That's why in May 2018 he bragged on Hugh Hewitt's right-wing radio program,

> What I want to do is make a lasting contribution to the country. And by appointing and confirming these strict constructionists to the courts who are in their late 40s or early 50s . . . we're making a generational change in our country that will be repeated over and over and over down through the years.[45]

In *Citizens United*, the five conservatives on the Supreme Court definitively transformed our political system with the assertion that campaign spending is First Amendment–protected speech. The ruling overturned campaign finance laws from 1908 all the way up to those passed after Nixon's scandals.

As I noted in my book *Unequal Protection*, Justice John Paul Stevens fumed in his *Citizens United* dissent that "Money is property; it is not speech.... These property rights are not entitled to the same protection as the right to say what one pleases."

Stevens, with the concurrence of Justices Ruth Bader Ginsburg, Stephen Breyer, and Sonia Sotomayor, wrote the dissenting opinion in the *Citizens United* case.

Quoting earlier Supreme Court cases and the founders, Stevens wrote:

> *The word "soulless" constantly recurs in debates over corporations.... Corporations, it was feared, could concentrate the worst urges of whole groups of men. Thomas Jefferson famously fretted that corporations would subvert the Republic.*

And, Stevens reasoned, the founders could not have possibly meant to confer First Amendment rights on corporations when they adopted the Constitution in 1787 and proposed the Bill of Rights in 1789, because "[a]ll general business corporation statutes appear to date from well after 1800." To make his point, Stevens even quoted Chief Justice John Marshall.

Sometimes referred to as the "father of the Supreme Court," Marshall had written in an early-19th-century decision text that Stevens quoted in his *Citizens United* dissent: "A corporation is an artificial being, invisible, intangible, and existing only in contemplation of law. Being a mere creature of law, it possesses only those properties which the charter of its creation confers upon it."

Stevens's dissent called out Roberts, Alito, Scalia, Thomas, and Kennedy for their corrupt behavior in the *Citizens United* ruling, which he said was "the height of recklessness to dismiss Congress' years of bipartisan deliberation and its reasoned judgment."

The dissenting justices argued that the majority's ruling wasn't merely wrong, in both a contemporary and a historical sense, but it was *dangerous*. The dissent was explicit, clear, and shocking in how bluntly the three most senior members of the Court (along with the newbie, Sotomayor) called out their colleagues, two of whom (Roberts and Alito) had just recently been appointed to the Court by President George W. Bush.

The dissenters noted that it was their five colleagues (and their friends in high places) who were clamoring for corporations to have personhood and free-speech rights, not the American people, who were the "listeners" of such speech: "It is only certain Members of this Court, not the listeners themselves, who have agitated for more corporate electioneering."

By having free-speech rights equal with those of people, Stevens argued, corporations will actually harm the "competition among ideas" that the framers envisioned when they wrote the First Amendment. "[W]hen corporations grab up the prime broadcasting slots on the eve of an election," he wrote, "they can flood the market with advocacy that bears little or no correlation to the ideas of natural persons or to any broader notion of the public good. The opinions of real people may be marginalized."

The result will be that more and more people will simply stop participating in politics (it's interesting to note how prominent a role the words rigged system played in the 2016 election), stop being informed about politics, and stop voting. Our democracy might wither and could even die.

> *When citizens turn on their televisions and radios before an election and hear only corporate electioneering, they may lose faith in their capacity, as citizens, to influence public policy. A Government captured by corporate interests, they may come to believe, will be neither responsive to their needs nor willing to give their views a fair hearing. The predictable result is cynicism and disenchantment: an increased perception that large spenders "call the tune" and a reduced willingness of voters to take part in democratic governance.*

Citizens United wasn't the first time the Supreme Court extended First Amendment protections beyond living, breathing human beings. In the 1978 case *First National Bank of Boston v. Bellotti*, the Court ruled that *corporations* have First Amendment rights. The ruling in *Bellotti* upheld a long tradition on the Court of recognizing personhood for corporations, which started in 1819 with *Dartmouth College v. Woodward* and extended all the way through the 1886 *Santa Clara County v. Southern Pacific Railroad Co.* to the 2010 *Citizens United v. Federal Election Commission*.

And in the 2014 case *McCutcheon v. Federal Election Commission*, the five conservatives on the Supreme Court struck down some of the individual spending limits in the Federal Election Campaign Act.

Each of these cases gave corporations direct, usable economic (and thus political) power over the people's elected representatives in Congress. Taken together, these Supreme

Court rulings fundamentally changed the US political system and opened it up to an unlimited amount of campaign spending from hidden sources.

On my radio program in 2015, I asked former president Jimmy Carter about his thoughts on these rulings that have permitted "unlimited money in politics." He told me and my listeners,

> It violates the essence of what made America a great country in its political system. Now it's just an oligarchy, with unlimited political bribery being the essence of getting the nominations for president or to elect the president. And the same thing applies to governors and US senators and Congress members. So now we've just seen a complete subversion of our political system as a payoff to major contributors, who want and expect and sometimes get favors for themselves after the election's over.[46]

The Supreme Court's rulings and reinterpretations of federal law fundamentally changed our political system, allowing "unlimited political bribery" reaching every level of government—from the president all the way down to local school boards.

Congress never passed a law allowing for unlimited political bribery. Instead, Congress passed numerous laws to rein in political corruption—and the Supreme Court neutered those laws.

And based on what Mitch McConnell told Hugh Hewitt in May 2018, politicians like McConnell have realized that the courts *ultimately are more powerful than Congress or the president.*

Rather than trying to make political change through legislation, McConnell knows that packing the courts with hardright friends of billionaires and big corporations will have a much more lasting effect than any legislative victory he may accomplish.

Throughout American history, the courts have gotten the final say on pretty much all legislation. And their review of new laws has exploded over the last 150 years, threatening not only our constitutional republic but also the fate of humanity.

The Constitution Afflicts the Afflicted and Comforts the Comfortable

Challenging any part of the Constitution evokes a response like you'd get challenging the Bible to a very religious person: "How could you dare such blasphemy? This is a *perfect* document."

Many Americans believe that our Constitution protects individual rights and creates a government that is, first and foremost, directed to operate in the realm of the common good (known in the Constitution as the "general welfare"). That's simply not the case.

In fact, through our 240-plus years of existence, there have only been a few eras when "democracy" was really playing out in a big way, if democracy means that the will of the majority of the people is what becomes law.

Most of the rest of the history of our nation is the history of a relatively small group of wealthy and powerful people riding roughshod over majorities or large minorities of our population.

*And that's why the Supreme Court—with a few exceptions—
most frequently sides with great wealth and the power attendant
to it.* That's the predictable consequence of a Constitution that
places property rights and the right to contract above most
everything else.

The Constitution Protects Property and Its Owners

For as long as it has existed, the Supreme Court has played
the principal role of defender of commercial and property
rights.

In the 1819 case of *Dartmouth College v. Woodward*, the
Supreme Court first discovered corporate rights in the US
Constitution.

The ruling overturned New Hampshire's reorganization of
Dartmouth College and kept it as a private institution. Justice
Marshall then asserted both the power of the Supreme Court
and the primacy of the private property represented by the
corporation that owned and ran Dartmouth.

And that's the system that the US Constitution set up.

Property is so deeply woven into our founding documents
that the Constitution could be seen, first and foremost, as a contract that protects the right to private property above all else.

The Supreme Court enforces that right of property. The
single clause of the Constitution that has generated the largest
number of Supreme Court cases and decisions over the years
has nothing to do with the rights to life, liberty, or the pursuit
of happiness.

Instead, it's been the Commerce Clause.[47]

The business of the United States has been, from its inception, business.

Article I, Section 8, not only establishes the power of Congress to regulate (and thus protect) commerce; it also establishes (along with other parts of the Constitution) numerous other property rights and protections. Some examples:

"To establish . . . uniform Laws on the subject of Bankruptcies throughout the United States" protects those people engaged in business, even if they end up screwing their customers or suppliers through their bankruptcy.

"To coin Money, regulate the Value thereof, and of foreign Coin, and fix the Standard of Weights and Measures" defines the economic ground in which an economy is rooted: a sound currency and standards that can be used in commerce.

"To define and punish Piracies and Felonies committed on the high Seas, and Offences against the Law of Nations" outlaws piracy and marine theft, activities that weighed heavily on wealthy ship owners and businesses that depended on the oceans and rivers to transport their goods to market. "To make Rules for the Government and Regulation of the land and naval Forces" does the same.

"To provide for calling forth the Militia to execute the Laws of the Union, suppress Insurrections and repel Invasions" would take care of rebellions forever, particularly if, as in the early years of our nation, they were protesting economic injustice.

Article I, Section 9, reads, "No Bill of Attainder or ex post facto Law shall be passed." This protected both property rights and the right of people to do things to make money that were nasty but not yet illegal.

"The Migration or Importation of such Persons as any of the States now existing shall think proper to admit, shall not be prohibited by the Congress prior to the Year one thousand eight hundred and eight, but a Tax or duty may be imposed on such Importation, not exceeding ten dollars for each Person" clearly defined the right of companies to engage in the slave trade with other nations clear into the next generation (1808).

Section 10 of Article I protects business and the wealthy from overzealous state legislatures while further defining federal authority: "No State shall enter into any Treaty, Alliance, or Confederation; grant Letters of Marque and Reprisal; coin Money; emit Bills of Credit; make any Thing but gold and silver Coin a Tender in Payment of Debts; pass any Bill of Attainder, ex post facto Law, or Law impairing the Obligation of Contracts."

Article III of the Constitution even went out of its way to protect the property rights of the blood relatives of people convicted of treason: "The Congress shall have Power to declare the Punishment of Treason, but no Attainder of Treason shall work Corruption of Blood, or Forfeiture except during the Life of the Person attainted."

In Article IV of the Constitution, state courts are required to honor the property rights defined or defended by courts in other states: "Full Faith and Credit shall be given in each State to the public Acts, Records, and judicial Proceedings of every other State."

Article IV, Section 2, makes it easy for Congress or a president to get rid of public lands but difficult to acquire them: "The Congress shall have Power to dispose of and make all needful Rules and Regulations respecting the Territory or other Property belonging to the United States; and nothing in this Constitution shall be so construed as to Prejudice any Claims of the United States, or of any particular State."

Even when time came to add a "Bill of Rights" to the Constitution in 1791, at least half of the rights protected were explicitly property rights:

- The Third Amendment bans government from using the private property of your home to stage or billet troops.

- The Fourth Amendment protects "houses, papers, and effects" from being seized by the government.

- The Fifth Amendment requires that your property be protected from government seizure, and if it is seized for the public good, you must be fairly compensated. In addition, it's explicit that "No person shall . . . be deprived of life, liberty, or property."

- The Seventh Amendment says that in all lawsuits "where the value in controversy shall exceed twenty dollars," property owners have an absolute right to trial by jury.

- The Eighth Amendment protects you from being wiped out by "excessive bail" should you be charged with a crime, protecting your wealth.

The Constitution wasn't principally written to protect human rights or the environment; it was written and ratified to protect wealth and business.

By 1888, the Constitution had done so little to protect average Americans that President Grover Cleveland said, in his fourth State of the Union Address to Congress:

> *The gulf between employers and the employed is constantly widening, and classes are rapidly forming, one comprising the very rich and powerful, while in another are found the toiling poor.*
>
> *As we view the achievements of aggregated capital, we discover the existence of trusts, combinations, and monopolies, while the citizen is struggling far in the rear or is trampled to death beneath an iron heel.*
>
> *Corporations, which should be the carefully restrained creatures of the law and the servants of the people, are fast becoming the people's masters.*[48]

With a few exceptions, typically lasting only a decade or two, the situation has only gotten worse, with the Supreme Court acting as an instrument and agent of the very wealthy and powerful in this nation.

The Constitution Protects Killers and Slave Owners

America was birthed from genocide. The slaughter of Native Americans was likely the greatest genocide in the history of the world.

Between 50 million and 100 million people were outright murdered or killed by European diseases over a 400-year period, and millions of the survivors were forcibly displaced from ancestral lands. So many people died that they left millions of acres of former farms fallow, and the regrowth of forests and jungles took so much carbon dioxide out of the air that it altered the world's weather for almost a century, producing "the Little Ice Age" of the 1600s.[49]

The Constitution protected the people and politicians who continued that genocide through the first 150 years of our nation's history. It's why "Indian Tribes" are mentioned three times in the Constitution, separating the people in those tribes from the laws, rights, and benefits of our country framed by the Constitution.

America was also birthed from slavery, and our Constitution was written to perpetuate that practice.

It's why the Constitution said, "No Person held to Service or Labour in one State, under the Laws thereof, escaping into another, shall, in Consequence of any Law or Regulation therein, be discharged from such Service or Labour, but shall be delivered up on Claim of the Party to whom such Service or Labour may be due."

Southern slave owners wanted everybody in the nation to help recapture any fugitives from their plantations. Northern states complied, because slavery was the single largest generator of cash for both the South and the North until the Civil War.[50]

It's also why the Constitution features the "three-fifths compromise," guaranteeing that, for purposes of federal representation, Southern states with large black populations could count three-fifths of their slaves as if they were citizen-voters. Because the number of enslaved persons was so great in the South, this "compromise" gave the South much more power in the House of Representatives and the Electoral College than if only free persons were counted.

The South not only had political power; it had enormous financial power. At the time of the Civil War, more than half the wealth of the slave states existed as human beings held in slavery, and the agricultural activity in those states was one of the main economic forces in the North.[51]

The North made so much money from the trade that a single slaving ship run generated the equivalent of nearly $30 million in today's dollars.[52]

Virtually *all* of this business was run out of New York City, and slave traders largely ran the city's political and social machines.

Immediately before the Civil War, between 1858 and 1860, more than 100 slave ships launched from the Port of New York. That's over $3 *billion* of revenue in just two years filling the vaults of businesses based in Manhattan. New York's slave ships outnumbered every other American city's even though the state of New York had outlawed slavery way back in 1827.[53]

A New Orleans newspaper editor wrote that if New York could no longer ship slaves to the South and Southern cotton to England, New York's "ships would rot at her docks; grass would grow in Wall Street and Broadway, and the glory of New York, like that of Babylon and Rome, would be numbered with the things of the past."[54]

When the Civil War broke out, New York Mayor Fernando Wood even proposed that New York City (Manhattan, Long

Island, and Staten Island) should join with the South in seced-ing from the rest of the United States. The new nation-state made up of the three islands would be called *Tri-Insula*.

The City Council was enthusiastic, but the war moved too quickly, so that when the bombing of Fort Sumter started, New York dropped its consideration of the idea of secession.

The power of slavery and cotton to generate wealth was foundational to our republic at its birth.

And slaves were considered the *property* of their owners.

When contemplating the end of the institution of slavery in the South, Patrick Henry, the largest slaveholder in Virginia, lamented that "in [such a] situation, I see a great deal of the property of the people of Virginia in jeopardy, and their peace and tranquility gone."

The Constitution Prefers Property Rights to Human Rights

In 2016, First Lady Michelle Obama addressed the Demo-cratic National Convention and caused a media firestorm with one simple statement: "I wake up every morning in a house that was built by slaves."

Michelle Obama was not alone waking up in a "house built by slaves." Every American wakes up in a country that was founded on stolen lands and built on the broken bodies of African slaves.

And our Constitution has guaranteed that we are never far from that history.

Between 19 and 41 of the 56 signers of the Declaration of Independence owned slaves at the time of the signing,[55] and representatives from the South threatened to scuttle the American then-confederacy in its infancy, depending on whether the new Constitution would see slaves as property or as persons.

Southern slaveholders feared that if slaves were taxed at the same rate as freed men, it would be economically impossible to maintain large plantations, and it would become cheaper to free their slaves.

Thomas Lynch raised this concern at the Continental Congress in 1776, declaring, "If it is debated, whether their Slaves are their Property, there is an End of the Confederation. Our Slaves being our Property, why should they be taxed more than the Land, Sheep, Cattle, Horses, &c."[56]

The founders' views hadn't evolved much by a decade later when the 13 states began to draft a new Constitution to replace the weak and ineffectual Articles of Confederation. In 1788, Patrick Henry worried that a federal slave tax might be so burdensome that it would "compel the Southern States to liberate their negroes."[57]

The Constitution Protects Takers, Not the Taken

The Fugitive Slave Clause presented the country with one of its earliest constitutional disputes, which began a simmering divide between the North and South that would eventually explode into the Civil War.

By 1791, it was clear to the South that the Fugitive Slave Clause pitted states' rights against property rights, but it was unclear which set of rights was superior.

The first challenge came from the state of Pennsylvania. Pennsylvania had passed a law in 1788—one year before the ratification of the US Constitution—saying that it was illegal to kidnap someone from Pennsylvania and force them into slavery in the South. The law provided some exceptions and processes for Southern slave owners to reclaim escaped slaves, if they could prove their case before a Pennsylvania magistrate.

In 1791, just two years after the ratification of the US Constitution, the governor of Pennsylvania, Thomas Mifflin, demanded that the governor of Virginia, Beverley Randolph, hand over three Virginians: Francis McGuire, Absalom Wells, and Baldwin Parsons.

Pennsylvania courts indicted the three for kidnapping an African American and taking him to Virginia to be enslaved. Justice Joseph Story wrote, "The governor of Virginia . . . referred the matter to the attorney-general of that state, who advised that the demand ought not to be complied with."[58]

The governors took the matters to President Washington. Mifflin wrote to Washington on July 18, 1791, "I have thought the present, a proper, occasion to bring the subject into your view, that, by the interposition of the Federal Legislature . . . such regulations may be established, as will, in future, obviate all doubt and embarrassment, upon a constitutional question, so delicate and important."[59]

Washington passed the matter to Congress, and in February 1793, he signed the first federal Fugitive Slave Act to deal with the "doubt and embarrassment" of the constitutional question.

The law seemed to work. The issue didn't escalate to the federal level for nearly 50 years, when the Supreme Court finally weighed in on the matter in 1842's *Prigg v. Pennsylvania* decision.

Edward Prigg was a bounty hunter hired to capture Margaret Morgan, a fugitive who had escaped from Maryland (a slave state) to Pennsylvania (a free state).

Prigg seized Morgan and her two children, dragging them before a Pennsylvania magistrate, who ruled that Prigg didn't have enough evidence to take his hostages to Maryland.

So Prigg tried to kidnap them, only to get himself arrested for breaking Pennsylvania's state laws about capturing people.

Justice John McLean delivered the sole dissent: "The state law is not violated by the seizure of the slave by the master, for this is authorized by the act of congress; but by removing him out of the state by force, and without proof of right, which the act does not authorize."

In other words, according to the dissent, the Constitution would allow Prigg to kidnap Margaret Morgan and her children—if he could prove to a magistrate that they were *really* fugitive slaves.

All of the other justices ruled that the Fugitive Slave Act of 1793 superseded Pennsylvania's state law, so the state had to permit Prigg to take his hostages to Maryland.

Many legal scholars have argued that the *Prigg* decision set a legal precedent that made 1857's *Dred Scott v. Sandford* decision nearly inevitable.[60]

With the Compromise of 1850 (which resolved the conflict over slave or free status for the states won in the Mexican-American War, as well as resolving the status of California and Utah), Congress passed a new Fugitive Slave Act, which tipped the scale further toward property rights over states' rights.

Among other stringent changes, the Fugitive Slave Act of 1850 set bounties for returning fugitives and fines for anyone who helped a fugitive, and penalties for judges and marshals who refused to hear cases.

The Fugitive Slave Clause spun a fundamental tension between property rights and states' rights in our Constitution—where human, civil, and environmental rights are continuously under attack.

This fundamental tension was so great that President Washington signed a more detailed law on how to deal with fugitive slaves between the states in 1793—10 years before the Court seized power with the *Marbury* decision. Nonetheless, the tension between property rights and states' rights festers, and it manifests every time a corporation sues a state over an environmental or consumer protection.

The Hidden History
of the People
and the Court

The Supreme Court's interpretations have changed just as much and as frequently as society itself in the United States.

Part 2 of this book explores how the Court has most often ruled against popular interests, and how Americans—from average Americans to the president—have fought back against the Court's most harmful rulings.

The Supreme Court versus Labor

At the time of the United States' founding in 1789, the country was agrarian. Work was done by manpower (often enslaved manpower) or by animal power. But by the time the United States broke out in civil war, the Industrial Revolution was already well under way.

The Industrial Revolution was just that: a revolution. Society fundamentally changed as machines replaced labor, as the cotton gin replaced enslaved people, and as factories sprouted up across the Northeast to produce finished goods at rates unachievable until then.

As new machines replaced slave power, a new group of nationwide property owners replaced the aristocratic slave owners in the South. These wealthy industrialists and bankers eventually seized so much power and wealth that they were collectively known as the "Robber Barons."

As the Robber Barons accumulated wealth, they turned that wealth toward capturing the American government.

The judiciary had always been the most conservative branch of government, but the Supreme Court became even more bonded and obedient to great wealth between the 1870s and 1900.

If the conservative philosophy held that *somebody* had to be in charge, the Supreme Court seemed pleased to allow the wealthiest leaders in American industry to be in charge. Because property rights were at the core of the Constitution, and those with the greatest wealth also owned the most "property," the Supreme Court, in most instances throughout our history, readily deferred to their wishes.

The transfer of wealth and power from Southern slave owners to Northern industrialists was reflected in the Court's rulings. No longer did slave rebellions threaten the flow of capital for America's wealthy elite: in the Gilded Age, the enemy of capital became labor.

The Court's rulings weakened labor at nearly every turn from the 1870s forward.

But even as the Court's opinion changed to uphold America's new class of elite property owners, the Court was also ruling with the popular opinion about labor. Many Americans in the 19th century were distrustful of organized labor and the new immigrants who supported it. It wasn't until the country plunged into the Great Depression that labor got a fair shake in both the court of public opinion and the Supreme Court.

The Court has in many ways elevated itself above the legislative and executive branches, but it is often still led by public opinion: this part of the book exposes how democratic demands have forced the Supreme Court to change its opinion in several notable instances throughout US history.

Haymarket and *Allgeyer*: The Public Turns against Labor and the Court Follows

No one knew who threw the bomb in Chicago's Haymarket Square on May 4, 1886.

The bomb's deafening explosion suddenly transformed Haymarket Square into a battlefield that pitted union workers against the Chicago Police Department.

By the end of the year, a grand jury indicted eight men for conspiracy for the Haymarket bombing. Evidence was thin, but anti-worker and anti-immigrant sentiment led the jury to find all eight men guilty. Seven of the men were sentenced to death, and one man was sentenced to 15 years at hard labor (still permitted under the 13th Amendment, which ended slavery *except* for people convicted of crimes).

The defendants appealed their sentences twice. First, they went to the Illinois Supreme Court, which upheld the original court's rulings. The defendants then entered a writ of error to the US Supreme Court. The US Supreme Court simply denied the writ of error, once again leaving the original decision intact.

The outcome was predictable. This was a Gilded Age, and America was fundamentally and rapidly transforming into an industrial nation. Former slaves and former sharecroppers flocked to the North for manufacturing and railway jobs. Those Americans were competing with an influx of immigrants from Germany and Eastern Europe, and so the industrialists held all the cards.

The glut of labor drove down wages and forced people to accept unsafe working conditions. Nativists blamed low wages and poor working conditions on immigrants and the influx of African Americans into urban areas.

The unions fought hard to improve conditions for workers (the gathering at Haymarket was in part to demand an eight-hour work day). But the economy was booming and (as today) many Americans didn't want to rock the boat: they were happy just to have a job, no matter how low-paid or unsafe.

And the Haymarket riot led Americans to associate the labor movement with "violent" anarchists and "un-American" socialist factions.

Eleven years after Haymarket, the Supreme Court delivered a massive blow to the labor movement in the 1897 *Allgeyer v. Louisiana* decision. The Court unanimously ruled in *Allgeyer* that the 14th Amendment right to liberty included the individuals' "liberty to contract."

With *Allgeyer*, the Supreme Court had essentially rendered unions powerless compared with property owners, employers, and industrialists.

The Court had also recently reinterpreted the 14th Amendment. Previously the Court had interpreted the 14th Amendment narrowly. But at the height of the Gilded Age in the late 19th century, the Supreme Court reinterpreted the Due Process Clause of the 14th Amendment to discover a "freedom of contract" between employer and employee.

The Court then expanded on the newfound freedom of contract to weaken unions, overturn minimum wage laws, and permit child labor.

Unions grew in strength for the next 40 years, picking up members by the thousands. But popular opinion didn't tip in the United States until 1929, when the country plunged into the Great Depression.

The Great Depression: The Public Embraces Labor and the Supreme Court Follows

For forty years after *Allgeyer*, the Lochner Court fully embraced its role as arbiter of what was constitutional and embraced its role as a legislator-of-last-resort that could simply reinterpret or nullify a law that Congress had passed.

With the onset of the Great Depression and the election of Franklin Delano Roosevelt, though, the judiciary and the executive were about to seriously clash for the first time in nearly a century.

Four of the justices, Pierce Butler, James Clark McReynolds, George Sutherland, and Willis Van Devanter, were collectively known as the Four Horsemen. They were invariably joined by one of the other justices to strike down New Deal legislation that attempted to address unemployment and poverty, no matter how popular it was.

The Four Horsemen claimed to be originalists or *strict constructionists* who somehow could read the founders' intent from the Constitution. The justices disregarded the historical reality that the founders were not of a single mind.

Interpretations from the Lochner era didn't reflect the Constitution's framers' 18th-century colonial understanding of the world; they reflected a 19th-century industrialist understanding of the world, steeped in social Darwinism. They pushed for "survival of the fittest" economics along with pseudoscientific rationales for racism and sexism.

Ideologically, these four justices were the predecessors of conservative ideologues on the Supreme Court such as Neil Gorsuch and Antonin Scalia. Economically, they embraced laissez-faire economics and rejected any federal powers that were not *explicitly* granted by the US Constitution.

For 40 years during the Lochner era, the Court struck down dozens of state laws protecting workers, including women and children. During the period between 1897 and 1929, the Court was ruling largely with the booming industrialist economy and saw the labor movement as disruptive rather than positive.

However, with the onset of the Great Depression, these industrialists lost the popular support they had enjoyed in the aftermath of the Haymarket bombing—but the ever-conservative Supreme Court had not caught up with popular opinion.

In 1935, the Supreme Court ruled that both the Agricultural Adjustment Act and the National Industrial Recovery Act were unconstitutional. The rulings gutted Roosevelt's New Deal legislation.

The Agricultural Adjustment Act had passed in 1933 with 73 percent of the House of Representatives voting for it. The bill passed the Senate with 64 percent of the Senate voting for it. After it was struck down, William Leuchtenburg wrote for *Smithsonian* magazine, "Many farmers were incensed. On the night following [Justice Owen] Roberts' opinion, a passerby in Ames, Iowa, discovered life-size effigies of the six majority opinion justices hanged by the side of a road."[1]

The National Industrial Recovery Act, with its famous "Blue Eagle" logo, had likewise passed with 80 percent of the House voting for it and 70 percent of senators voting for it.

When the Supreme Court used its power of judicial review to overturn these laws, it wasn't viewed just as an assault on FDR's New Deal. It was, in the opinion of many Americans (and FDR himself), an assault on the very basis of our democratic republic.

But they were federal laws, and supporters of the Court's decisions argued that the laws in question were not in the realm of the federal government. If those laws were passed by states, supporters of the Court argued, the Supreme Court would allow them to stand as constitutional.

Then, shortly before Roosevelt was reelected in 1936, the Court struck down a New York *state* law that established a minimum wage for women and children in *Morehead v. New York ex rel. Tipaldo*. The pendulum of popular opinion swung against the Court almost overnight. One Republican newspaper in New York declared its opposition to the ruling: "The law that would jail any laundryman for having an underfed horse should jail him for having an underfed girl employee."[2]

And as historian David B. Woolner, author of *The Last 100 Days: FDR at War and at Peace*, noted, "Over . . . 13 months, the court struck down more pieces of legislation than at any other time in U.S. history."[3]

In 1937, the National Labor Relations Act and the Social Security Act were on their way to the Court. Considering how the Four Horsemen had ruled during FDR's first term, Roosevelt knew that he needed to do something or risk losing both pieces of legislation.

If the Court overturned both acts, the New Deal would be dead on the bench.

FDR Tries to Pack the Supreme Court

With the New Deal on the line, Roosevelt went on the attack. On February 5, 1937, just months after his landslide reelection, he announced his plan. He asked Congress for the authority to appoint one justice for each justice over 70 who would not retire.

In 1937, the average life expectancy for men in the United States was only 58 years old.[4] The average age of the Supreme Court justices at the time was 71 years old, and six of the justices were 70 years or older. A book mocking the Court, called *The Nine Old Men*, "was rapidly moving up the bestseller lists."[5]

Roosevelt's plan took advantage of that public opinion that the age of the justices was negatively affecting the Court's decision making along with the Court's ability to quickly rule on cases.

FDR directly called into question the "capacity of the judges themselves" to dispose of the growing number of cases facing federal courts. The United States' population had nearly doubled between 1900 and 1936, and the number of cases facing federal court dockets had exploded. Citizens were waiting longer and longer to go in front of older and older judges.

Roosevelt's plan would have immediately given him six appointments to the Supreme Court and up to 44 appointments for federal lower courts. Roosevelt argued that "a constant and systematic addition of younger blood will vitalize the courts."

On March 9, 1937, Roosevelt told the nation that the Court was ruling not just against himself and Congress, but against the will of the American people, themselves.

> *Last Thursday I described the American form of Government as a three horse team provided by the Constitution to the American people so that their field might be plowed. The three horses are, of course, the three branches of government—the Congress, the Executive and the Courts.*

Two of the horses are pulling in unison today; the third is not. Those who have intimated that the President of the United States is trying to drive that team, overlook the simple fact that the President, as Chief Executive, is himself one of the three horses.

It is the American people themselves who are in the driver's seat. It is the American people themselves who want the furrow plowed.

It is the American people themselves who expect the third horse to pull in unison with the other two [emphasis mine]."

"The Courts," Roosevelt boomed, "have cast doubts on the ability of the elected Congress to protect us against catastrophe by meeting squarely our modern social and economic conditions."[6]

Roosevelt's critics were aghast at his plans. They claimed he was trying the "pack the Court" with justices who would simply be his yes men.

Reacting to his critics, Roosevelt cut to the heart of the matter:

[I]f by that phrase the charge is made . . . that I will appoint Justices who will not undertake to override the judgment of the Congress on legislative policy, that I will appoint Justices who will act as Justices and not as legislators—if the appointment of such Justices can be called "packing the Courts," then I say that I and with me the vast majority of the American people favor doing just that thing—now.

Congress never voted on the plan. It's unclear whether it would have succeeded, or if a more moderate plan that would have given him only two or three justices might have succeeded.

On March 29, 1937, a Washington State minimum wage law came before the Supreme Court in *West Coast Hotel Co. v. Parrish*. The law in question was nearly identical to the New York State law that that had come before the Court a year earlier. But this time, Justice Owen Roberts abandoned the Four Horsemen to uphold Washington State's minimum wage law in a 5–4 decision.

In a series of 5–4 decisions two weeks later, the Court upheld the National Labor Relations Act as constitutional. The ruling was astonishing.

Labor Secretary Frances Perkins was close friends with Justice Roberts's wife, Elizabeth. When the decisions came down, according to Perkins's biographer Kirstin Downey, "she rushed that afternoon to Roberts' home" and "threw her arms around the man and hugged him."

"Owen, I'm so proud of you," Perkins told the Supreme Court justice. "A man of your standing and intelligence who is not afraid to change his mind!"

Downey wrote of how Roberts was embarrassed by the affection but also very pleased. "Really, do you think so?" he replied to Perkins.

Less than two months later, the Court declared that Social Security was constitutional.

The New Deal had been saved from execution on the Supreme Court's bench. Social Security had been salvaged and the National Labor Relations Act gave labor and unions a lifeline after 40 years of fighting to stay afloat.

Shortly after the Supreme Court upheld Social Security, Willis Van Devanter, one of the Four Horsemen, retired from his position after 26 years on the bench. This gave Roosevelt his first Supreme Court pick: Hugo Black. Less than a year later, Roosevelt got his second pick when Justice George Sutherland announced that he was retiring. By the end of his 12-year presidency, Roosevelt ended up appointing nine new members to fill eight of the nine seats on the Supreme Court (one, James Byrnes, served just a year and a half and was then replaced by FDR).

Roberts's about-face in *West Coast Hotel* was referred to at the time as "the switch in time that saved nine."

But despite the catchy phrase to describe Roberts's switch, the relationship between Roberts's vote and Roosevelt's plan is not clear.

Historians argue over why Roberts switched and whether he was already planning to switch his vote on these cases before Roosevelt introduced his plan to pack the Court. They also argue over why the Democratic-controlled Senate buried Roosevelt's court-packing bill in July 1937.

At the beginning of 1937, the American people were overwhelmingly supportive of Roosevelt, Congress, and the New Deal. At the same time, the American people showed nothing but contempt toward the Supreme Court for "legislating from the bench."

Justice Roberts's flip in 1937 is just one instance of the Supreme Court making an about-face to reflect public opinion, once public opinion hit a critical mass.

The Court Devastates Union Rights

Although the Court swung in 1937 toward support of FDR's New Deal—including its support of the right of workers to organize into unions—that support was short-lived. They supported labor in two cases in 1937, and again in 1944. But 1944 was also the year that the Court turned, as FDR was ailing and the world was at war.

Although the GOP initially embraced unions, by the time of FDR's death it was clear to the Republican Party that unions would only help Democrats and hurt Republicans, particularly in their effort to regularly have a Republican president who could feed reliable right-wingers for nomination to the Supreme Court.

Probably sensing this, they began inventing new doctrines that didn't exist in law in 1944 in *Steele v. Louisville & Nashville Railroad Co.*, coming up with the notion that unions must provide "fair representation" and then determining for themselves what "fair" meant.

In the nearly 80 years since then, the Court has come up with over a dozen new regulations on unions that don't exist in law, and Republicans in the House, Senate, and White House have, at various times throughout, rebuffed any Democratic efforts to repeal Taft-Hartley or put into law union regulations that would defy the Supreme Court.

The viciously anti-union Taft-Hartley ("Right to Work") Act passed Congress over Harry Truman's veto in 1949, and the Court has been on a tear ever since, destroying union rights step-by-step, particularly since Ronald Reagan elevated the GOP war on labor to a core doctrine for his party.

To hasten the process, a group of wealthy businessmen and inherited-wealth billionaires (the Walton family among others) funded the establishment, in 1968, of the National Right to Work Committee (NRTWC) and its 501(c)(3) foundation to bring cases to the Supreme Court so they could rule against unions. Most of the cases that have had truly devastating impact on unions since the mid-1970s were the result of NRTWC's efforts.

There's an entire analysis of each of these cases, with footnotes, describing what rights the Court removed from working people and how and when they did it, on my website, titled "Overturning Child Labor in the United States."[7]

The Supreme Court versus Civil Rights

In 1870, Massachusetts Senator Charles Sumner introduced a bill that would become the nation's first major piece of civil rights legislation. The law guaranteed "that all persons within the jurisdiction of the United States shall be entitled to the full and equal enjoyment of the accommodations, advantages, facilities, and privileges of inns, public conveyances on land or water, theaters, and other places of public amusement; . . . and applicable alike to citizens of every race and color, regardless of any previous condition of servitude."

Sumner's Civil Rights Act set out to profoundly change America's public spaces by banning racial discrimination.

Four years after it was first introduced, Sumner was on his deathbed. He begged those at his bedside, including Frederick Douglass, to make sure the bill passed.[8]

The bill finally passed with a 38 to 26 vote in the Senate on February 27, 1875.[9] It went into effect on March 1, 1875.

And less than 10 years later, the Civil Rights Act of 1875 was overturned by the Supreme Court in 1883 on the basis that it infringed on states' rights under the 10th Amendment, and that the 14th Amendment applied only to federal and state governments, not to individuals.

Justice John Marshall Harlan saw that the Court was undermining the will of Congress and the states that had ratified the three anti-slavery (13th, 14th, and 15th) amendments, and heaped criticism on the other justices for bowing to powerful individuals and leaving the door open for future discrimination by corporate bosses. He wrote,

> My brethren admit that [the 13th Amendment] established and decreed universal civil freedom throughout the United States. But did the freedom thus established involve nothing more than exemption from actual slavery? Was nothing more intended than to forbid one man from owning another as property? . . . Today it is the colored race which is denied, by corporations and individuals wielding public authority, rights fundamental in their freedom and citizenship. At some future time, it may be that some other race will fall under the ban of race discrimination.[10]

Harlan also expressed grave concern that the ruling undermined the national government itself, pointing out that "this court has uniformly held that the national government has the power, whether expressly given or not, to secure and protect rights conferred or guaranteed by the Constitution."[11]

Nonetheless, the Court struck down the Civil Rights Act of 1875. The Court ruled in favor of "states' rights" and in favor of allowing "corporations and individuals wielding public authority," as Harlan put it, to discriminate against American citizens.

Thirteen years after the Court tossed Sumner's Civil Rights Act, the Court gave birth to legal apartheid with its ruling in *Plessy v. Ferguson*.

"Separate but Equal": Created by the Court, Ended through Popular Struggle

Liberal supporters of the Court's ability to rewrite the nation's laws often point to *Brown v. Board of Education* as an example of why it's good that the Supreme Court can act as the final arbiter of society in America. But the truth is, the Supreme Court's 1954 ruling in *Brown* only *undid* damage that the Court had needlessly wrought when it reinterpreted the 14th Amendment in *Plessy*.

If not for a century of coordinated and strategic efforts to end segregation in America, there might well still be laws on the books that enforce segregation in the United States as a result of that original ruling in the 19th century.

In 1935, Charles Hamilton Houston was the special counsel for the National Association for the Advancement of Colored People (NAACP). In a 1936 essay titled "Don't Shout Too Soon," Houston made it clear that changing the laws was only step one in the struggle for equality. "Lawsuits mean little unless supported by public opinion," he asserted, "Nobody needs to explain to the Negro the difference between the law in books and the law in action."[12]

Far from ending segregation in practice, the *Brown* ruling only opened the door for thousands of individual legal challenges to be filed against thousands of individual segregated school districts.

But at least the law on the books had changed.

And the only reason the law on the books had changed was because a determined group of citizens, many attorneys among them, organized and fought legal battle after legal battle for over a century between 1848 and 1954.

The Road to *Plessy*

The first notable case to challenge school segregation in the United States only reached as far as the Massachusetts Supreme Court in 1849. The case was *Roberts v. City of Boston*, commonly called "the *Roberts* case."

A black printer named Benjamin Roberts had filed a lawsuit against the city of Boston. The schools near his home denied his five-year-old daughter, Sarah, admission. Nevertheless, Sarah tried to go to the nearest school on a cold February day, only to be promptly ejected by a teacher.

Two attorneys took the case. One of the attorneys was Robert Morris, one of the first black lawyers in the nation at a time when many black Americans still lived in literal chains. The other attorney was a young Charles Sumner, eventual leader of the radical anti-slavery Republicans and author of the ill-fated Civil Rights Act of 1875.

The *Roberts* case was heard in Massachusetts 15 years before the 14th Amendment passed, and nearly 50 years before the Supreme Court ruled in *Plessy* that "separate but equal" did not violate the 14th Amendment. Sumner anticipated the argument in the *Roberts* case, though, and he argued to the court,

> *This consideration cannot be neglected, the matters taught in the two schools may be precisely the same;* but a school exclusively devoted to one class, must differ essentially in spirit and character from that Common School known to the law, where all classes meet together in Equality *[emphasis mine].*[13]

Sumner's argument mirrored that of the NAACP in the early part of the 20th century in the lead-up to *Brown*. But it did not convince the justices of the Massachusetts Supreme Court, and the court ruled against Benjamin Roberts and his daughter, forbidding her from attending Boston's whites-only public schools.

Massachusetts Chief Justice Lemuel Shaw delivered the opinion of the court, and he agreed "in the fullest manner, that colored persons, the descendants of Africans, are entitled by law, in this commonwealth, to equal rights, constitutional and political, civil and social."

Shaw then added, "The question then arises, whether the regulation in question, which provides separate schools for colored children, is a violation of any of these rights."

He concluded that the court couldn't do anything about it, because the issue was *not one of law on the books*, but one of *public opinion*. "It is urged," Shaw declared, "that this maintenance of separate schools tends to deepen and perpetuate the odious distinction of caste, founded in a deep-rooted prejudice in public opinion. This prejudice, if it exists, is not created by law, and probably cannot be changed by law."[14]

Defeated by the state court, Roberts and Sumner took the matter to the Massachusetts legislature, and in 1855, Massachusetts finally banned segregated schools in the state.

The case never made it to the Supreme Court, so the story of *Roberts* should end there. But instead, the 1849 ruling in the *Roberts* case established a precedent that *segregation did not violate equality*. In 1896, that precedent was used in *Plessy v. Ferguson* to reinterpret the 14th Amendment, birthing the modern era of Jim Crow under the logic of "separate but equal."

Charles Houston and the Long Slog to End Jim Crow

Charles Hamilton Houston was central to the struggle, even though he died before the *Brown* case made it to the Supreme Court.[15]

Houston was born in Washington, DC, just one year before *Plessy* put "separate but equal" into the law books; his father worked as a printer and his mother as a seamstress. Their customers were congressmen, military brass, and other movers and shakers in the nation's capital.

Houston grew up in the upper crust of Jim Crow America's second-tier caste, and he spearheaded the end of Jim Crow.

His performance at the nation's first black high school earned Houston a partial scholarship to Amherst College as the university's only black student.

After Houston graduated from Amherst at the top of his class, he returned to Washington, DC. There, he taught at Howard University as a professor of English and of "Negro Literature"—until the United States entered World War I in 1917.

Houston joined the army when the war started because he calculated that it would be better to volunteer as a black officer than to be drafted as an enlisted man of any color.

During his time at Fort Des Moines (the country's first training camp for black officers), Houston quickly learned that Jim Crow held rank in the army: black Americans were still treated as distinctly second class, regardless of rank.

Houston's camp commander at Fort Des Moines once wrote in a report that black soldiers lacked "mental potential and higher qualities of character essential to command and leadership."

Historian Douglas Linder found evidence in Houston's letters that his time in the army impassioned him in his lifelong fight to end segregation and discrimination in America.

Houston declared in one letter, "I made up my mind that I would never get caught again without knowing something about my rights; that if luck was with me, and I got through this war, I would study law and use my time fighting for men who could not strike back."[16]

Upon Houston's return to America in 1919, he immediately faced discrimination aboard a train, and he wrote, "I felt damned glad I had not lost my life fighting for this country." He left the army two months later in April, announcing, "My battleground is in America, not France."[17]

Houston aimed specifically to overturn the 1896 Court ruling in *Plessy*, which established a federal legal precedent of "separate but equal." Homer Plessy and his attorneys had staged the whole event, and they never seriously considered that they might lose in the Supreme Court.[18]

Having learned from *Plessy*, the lawyers aiming to overturn *Plessy* needed to be sure that they wouldn't make the situation worse through *another* undesirable Supreme Court ruling.

In 1930, Houston and the NAACP devised a plan, laid out in the *Margold Report*.

The plan, to chip away at *Plessy* without challenging the ruling directly, would ensure that the stakes would be reasonable in any given case, and each case would work toward establishing a broader framework of precedents that would eventually replace "separate but equal." (In his infamous memo, Lewis Powell advised the business community to take a similar approach to secure a right-wing stranglehold on America.)

Brown was the culmination of three decades of test cases and legal challenges brought forward by citizens and the NAACP.

The losses were frequent, but the wins chipped away at "separate but equal," from *Pearson et al. v. Murray State University*, which kicked open the admission for black students to the University of Maryland School of Law, to *Sweatt v. Painter* and *McLaurin v. Oklahoma State Regents*, which ended "separate but equal" at the graduate and professional school levels.

When Houston died at 54 years old, he had trained a new generation of black attorneys, including future Supreme Court

Justice Thurgood Marshall. After Houston's death, the next generation of black attorneys continued to file legal challenges that chipped away at Jim Crow one ruling at a time.

Brown: The Supreme Court Overrules Itself

The Court's ruling in *Brown v. Board of Education*, and Thurgood Marshall's win in the case, resulted from a decades-long effort that systematically challenged the Supreme Court's unjust ruling in *Plessy*.

In general, liberal observers support the Court's ruling in *Brown* as a corrective ruling; conservative observers object that the Court overstepped its bounds with a "coercive" interpretation of federal law.

Brown was really four cases bundled together. Chief Justice Earl Warren explained, "They are premised on different facts and different local conditions, but a common legal question justifies their consideration together in this consolidated opinion."[19]

Justice Marshall first presented arguments on the case on December 9, 1952, but the Supreme Court did not issue a decision until May 17, 1954—over 17 months later.

In his opinion on the Court's unanimous decision, Chief Justice Warren explained the futility of originalism on the matter:

> *The most avid proponents of the post-War Amendments undoubtedly intended them to remove all legal distinctions among "all persons born or naturalized in the United States." Their opponents, just as certainly, were antagonistic to both the letter and the spirit of the Amendments and*

wished them to have the most limited effect. What others in Congress and the state legislatures had in mind cannot be determined with any degree of certainty.[20]

Extending the precedents set in *Sweatt* and *McLaurin*, Warren states plainly, "We have now announced that such segregation is a denial of the equal protection of the laws."[21]

In a 9–0 decision, the *Brown* ruling tore "separate but equal" from the law books. But, as Charles Houston warned 20 years before, "Lawsuits mean little unless supported by public opinion."[22]

Even today, the United States is still wrestling to end institutional discrimination, from predatory and racist car and housing loans, to school districts that are still functionally segregated, to systemic income disparities, to racist policing that kills more black Americans and also sends them to jail more often and for longer sentences than white Americans.

The Court overturned *Plessy* only because bold attorneys like Thurgood Marshall and Charles Houston spent decades challenging different aspects of "separate but equal." They lost frequently. But over time, they built a body of precedent that forced the Court to overturn *Plessy*.

How *Roe* Empowered the Right

A few years before the 1973 *Roe v. Wade* decision, a phone call cut through the night's silence. The call woke Lewis Powell, then a lawyer in private practice. On the other end was a 19-year-old who worked for Powell's law firm, Hunton & Williams.

At the young man's desperate request, Powell left his home and met the midnight caller at his office, where he learned that the young man had been involved with an older divorcée, who was now dead.

The woman, who had been pregnant, wanted to have an abortion rather than endure the social crisis of having an out-of-wedlock child with a 19-year-old.

Abortions were against the law and thus unavailable in Virginia, so she asked the law firm's young courier to help. The boy messed up the procedure, and she hemorrhaged. She died in the boy's rented room, down the street from Powell's office.

In that era, many women died from unsterile, underground, or do-it-yourself procedures. When Powell met with his young employee, the police knew how the woman had died but still weren't sure who did it.

Powell took pity and used his outsized influence as a renowned attorney to meet *that night* with the local prosecutor, who was a friend. After talking with Powell, the prosecutor notified the police that he was not going to press charges.

Richard Nixon appointed Powell to the Supreme Court just a year or so later, in 1971. Two years later, the Supreme Court, in one of the most divisive rulings in US history, ruled on the question of abortion, with Powell voting to make it legal.

For liberals, the decision was an important step for women's rights, granting a constitutional basis for a woman's right to make decisions about her body. For conservatives, it represented "legislating from the bench" at its worse. For social conservatives, Catholics, and the religious right, *Roe* was a miscarriage of justice on par with *Dred Scott*.

The FDA approved birth control pills for sale in 1960, and by 1965 they were in wide use with few complications and over 99 percent efficacy. Women could now choose when (or if) to get pregnant, and in turn they demanded equal workplace and educational rights.

The pill also kicked off the "sexual revolution" of the mid-1960s and 1970s, with "free love" sweeping the country among young people. Along with all that sex came a lot of unintended pregnancies—and a huge demand for abortion.

Most people old enough to remember the late 1960s and early 1970s recall young women occasionally going into the hospital for D&C procedures, an abbreviation for dilation and curettage, the opening of the cervix and removal of the uterine lining. If there was a fertilized egg implanted on that lining, it came out along with the uterine tissue. This was a generally safe method for girls to get abortions, if their parents could afford the hospital and a friendly family doctor would certify that the girl was having "difficult periods" and thus needed the D&C procedure.

But for most women in the United States, options were far more limited and far more dangerous.

The Supreme Court took the case because it recognized the growing number of young women dying from illegal procedures, and the class issues involved.

Abortion isn't mentioned in the Constitution, and it's hardly mentioned in any of the nonmedical literature of that era. With no constitutional foundation, the Court had to find some basis on which to decide the case.

Nixon appointee Justice Harry Blackmun wrote the lengthy decision in *Roe* with help from his old friend (and fellow Nixon appointee) William Rehnquist.

The Court decided, 6–3, to base its decision primarily on a woman's right to privacy, derived from both the 9th and 14th Amendments. Blackmun wrote,

> *This right of privacy, whether it be founded in the Fourteenth Amendment's concept of personal liberty and restrictions upon state action, as we feel it is, or, as the District Court determined, in the Ninth Amendment's reservation of rights to the people, is broad enough to encompass a woman's decision whether or not to terminate her pregnancy. The detriment that the State would impose . . . by denying this choice altogether is apparent.*

And with that decision, the Court lit a match to a stick of political dynamite.

The United States had not been the only country where abortion was illegal. It was against the law in Ireland, for example, a country that was 78 percent Catholic. The Irish were so opposed to abortion that in 1983 they even added a ban on it to their constitution. (The birth control pill was legalized in Ireland in 1980.)

But Ireland's Supreme Court didn't overturn that country's laws against abortion. The people did, in 2018. By referendum, they chose to amend their constitution to include the absolute right of women to seek safe and legal abortions, and for doctors to perform them.

Even those who strongly support "a woman's right to choose" (including this author) often wonder out loud—

given how rapidly women's rights were moving in the 1960s and early 1970s in the United States—how long it would have taken for most states, and eventually the entire nation, to legalize abortion through the legislative process.

Had this happened, it's likely that the murders of several abortion doctors wouldn't have occurred, and the country may well have been spared the pain and spectacle of years of public harassment of family planning clinics, because the legislative process around hot-button social issues involves public hearings and testimony and usually resolves into law only when there's majority public opinion in favor of it.

By short-circuiting this process, the Court handed religious zealots and right-wing hustlers like Randall Terry, Jerry Falwell, and Ted Cruz the keys to millions of dollars and a national platform.

Whether the ruling was proper, legally sound, or even appropriate in terms of saving women's lives is arguable to this day, although, as even Lewis Powell knew in 1973, legal abortions unequivocally save women's lives.

But by taking on a legislative process—right down to defining the three trimesters of a pregnancy and prescribing specific rules for abortion in each separately (done later in *Planned Parenthood v. Casey*)—the Court unquestionably went beyond anything the framers of the Constitution considered for its role.

And, in the process, its decision may well have led directly to the situation extant in 2019 where, in many Republican-controlled states, women are again dying from illegal and do-it-yourself abortions.

The Supreme Court and the Environment

From the founding of this republic until the 1960s, there wasn't a substantial concern about the environment, even as pollution from the Industrial Revolution poisoned millions of people worldwide.

After Lake Erie died and the Cuyahoga River caught on fire 13 times and Rachel Carson in 1962 published *Silent Spring*, warning of the threat of DDT to bird life (among other environmental concerns), Congress finally first addressed the environment in a serious way with the creation of the Environmental Protection Agency in December 1970.

It seems odd that Congress would have largely ignored the environment until the 172nd year of the United States' existence. But, as mentioned earlier, the hot new idea that animated the Enlightenment and the founding generation was the notion that individuals who weren't born to royalty or riches could nonetheless own things.

It was all about *property rights*. But in the modern era, environmental changes are destroying more and more property across our country—through drought, floods, severe storms, and wildfires—and concerns about property and the environment are colliding faster than ever.

So, how could the Supreme Court recognize the "rights of nature" when those rights (which are at the forefront of most indigenous peoples' laws and religion) weren't considered or discussed by the founders or by Congress for most of this nation's existence?

One frame would be to consider the constitutional provisions for the "general welfare" of the people. If a person is being poisoned, his welfare is at risk, along with his life. Even a considerable annoyance could be a harm.

The basis for this frame can be easily found in today's zoning regulations.

Local Zoning Law as Early Environmental Law

On November 18, 1731, the aldermen of New York City passed an ordinance banning the "slaughter of any Neat (cows and oxen bred for meat) Cattle" in the city. The penalty was 20 shillings, paid "one half thereof to the Informer and the Other half to the Treasurer of this City."

The Supreme Court took up the issue in the 1926 case of *Village of Euclid v. Ambler Realty Company.* That ruling established the absolute right of communities to define zoning restrictions for the public good and the good of the community itself.

As Justice George Sutherland wrote, "Building zone laws are of modern origin. The ordinance under review, and all similar laws and regulations, must find their justification in some aspect of the police power, asserted for the public welfare."

In 1954, the city of Chicago was being poisoned by "industrial solids and flue dust" from Republic Steel's factory on the Calumet River, which was a major artery and source of drinking water for the city. With no environmental law to draw on, the city's lawyers referred to the Rivers and Harbors Act of 1899. The pollutants were accumulating on and raising the river's bottom, the lawyers argued, and thus "created an 'obstruction' to the 'navigable capacity' of the river."

They won their case in federal court in 1954. In 1960, Republic Steel took the case to the Supreme Court, which upheld the lower court's ruling in *United States v. Republic Steel Corp.*

In 1955, Congress passed the first anti-pollution law, which provided money to the US Public Health Service to research pollution. The Supreme Court looked to this 1955 law to inform its decision in the 1960 case *Huron Portland Cement Co. v. City of Detroit.* In that case, the Court ruled that Detroit's anti-air-pollution law regulating smokestacks was constitutional.

Justice Potter Stewart noted in his decision that the Constitution,

> *conferring upon Congress the regulation of commerce, . . . never intended to cut the States off from legislating on all subjects relating to the health, life, and safety of their citizens, though the legislation might indirectly affect the commerce of the country. Legislation . . . may affect commerce and persons engaged in it without constituting a regulation of it, within the meaning of the Constitution.*[23]

Word was spreading. On August 29, 1962, a reporter asked President John F. Kennedy if the Public Health Service would investigate regulating pesticides.

"Yes, and I know that they already are," Kennedy replied. "I think particularly, of course, since Miss Carson's book, but they are examining the matter."[24]

Rachel Carson published *Silent Spring* a month later, in September 1962.

After years of debate, and only after the creation of the EPA, DDT was banned on June 2, 1972.

This was all part of a larger trend throughout the 1960s and 1970s of local and state governments passing their own air and water quality laws, in many cases using the same legal reasoning that was at the basis for zoning laws.

Protecting the Environment Goes Federal

By 1970, the hodgepodge of state and local laws had become a massive headache for industry. And Edmund Muskie was leading the Democratic field to challenge Nixon in the 1972 election.

In Muskie's own words, "Nixon saw me emerging as a potential presidential candidate and he knew of my interest in environmental issues, so he created the EPA. He tried to pre-empt the issue from me."[25]

Thus, in a shrewd political maneuver, Nixon signed the bill to create the Environmental Protection Agency in 1970.

As Nixon told Chrysler's Lee Iocacca and Henry Ford II, captured on the White House tapes on April 27, 1971, "[W]e are fighting, frankly, a delaying action. . . . [W]e can't have a completely safe society or safe highways or safe cars and pollution-free and so forth. Or we could go back and live like a bunch of damned animals. . . . [A]nd boy, this is true. It's true in, in the environmentalists and in the consumerism people. They're a group of people that aren't one really damn bit interested in safety or clean air. What they're interested in is destroying the system. They're enemies of the system."

To restrict the EPA, he put it under the control of the Office of Management and Budget (OMB), which had the power to severely restrict its funding by applying a cost-benefit analysis to every significant expenditure.[26]

Nixon was no environmentalist; he danced to the tune of industry whenever possible. For example, Congress passed a serious environmental law that threatened to reduce the profits of polluting industries, the Federal Water Pollution Control Act Amendments of 1972, which became commonly known as the Clean Water Act. Nixon promptly vetoed it.

Congress overrode his veto, and so Nixon ordered his EPA administrator not to use the full funding that the law appropriated for water cleanup and enforcement against industry. Congress erupted in protest, with the *New York Times'* Tom Wicker referring to Nixon's "imperial Presidency."[27]

After a landslide reelection victory, Nixon held a press conference on January 31, 1973, and rolled out the trope that now characterizes most industry-funded political actions against the environment. "The constitutional right of the President of the United States," Nixon said, "to not spend money, when the spending of money would mean either increasing prices or increasing taxes for the people—that right is absolutely clear."

The Supreme Court didn't settle the matter until one year after Nixon resigned. In 1975's *Train v. City of New York*, Justice Byron White wrote for the majority that the money had to be distributed under the Water Pollution Control Act, and under any law passed by Congress with a "firm commitment of substantial sums within a relatively limited period of time in an effort to achieve an early solution of what was deemed an urgent problem."[28]

Over the next four-plus decades, the EPA's power waxed and waned, limited often by its own administrator.

For instance, probably among the worst EPA administrators in the agency's history was Anne Gorsuch, the mother of current Supreme Court Justice Neil Gorsuch. She served under Reagan from May 1981 until she resigned in disgrace in March 1983, much as Scott Pruitt did from the Trump administration in 2018.

Like Pruitt, Gorsuch did not believe that the agency should exist, and so she slashed the agency's budget by 22 percent immediately upon taking office. Over her short tenure, enforcement cases dropped by 79 percent.[29] Friends of the Earth founder Joe Browder noted that her most lasting impact was "making anti-environmentalism one of the 10 commandments of being a Republican."[30]

While presidents Clinton and Obama both had a decided pro-environment tilt, at least one house of Congress was in Republican hands for much of their tenures, which limited what the EPA could do.

And in 1999, Bill Clinton's EPA, apparently under pressure from Clinton's corporate donors, refused to regulate greenhouse gases, saying that such regulation was beyond its powers granted by Congress in the Clean Air Act. The EPA said explicitly that it lacked the authority, and even if it did have the authority, doing so would "interfere with the President's more comprehensive approach" and could "hamper the President's ability to persuade developing countries to limit greenhouse gas emissions. Most important, they said, "there is uncertainty regarding the link between greenhouse gases and global warming."[31]

Governor Mitt Romney's state of Massachusetts sued Clinton's EPA under Section 202(a)(1) of the Clean Air Act, which says the EPA can regulate "air pollutants" from new motor vehicles, if the EPA judges those motor vehicles to "cause, or contribute to, air pollution which may reasonably be anticipated to endanger public health or welfare."

The lawsuit claimed that this section empowered the EPA to regulate greenhouse gases, because global warming would "endanger public health or welfare."[32]

Justice John Paul Stevens delivered the majority opinion in 2007, with the Court deciding in *Massachusetts v. EPA* that the EPA did, in fact, have the power to regulate greenhouse gases. But the Court didn't explicitly conclude that greenhouse gases endangered "public health or welfare."

Justices Roberts, Thomas, Scalia, and Alito dissented vigorously (pointing to that lack of "public health or welfare" finding), but they were still in the minority.

Massachusetts v. EPA is one of the few consequential Supreme Court decisions that served to protect the environment, and both Justice Alito and Justice Thomas have called for it to be overturned.[33]

The Planet's Future on Trial

It could be "the trial of the century," at least according to the government's attorneys who are trying to stop it, and it will almost certainly end up before the Supreme Court.

While there has been no shortage of lawsuits that peripherally involve climate change (such as the *Massachusetts v.*

EPA 5–4 decision), none up to this writing have litigated the scientific details of climate change in a way that could force the federal government to take clear and specific action to cut greenhouse gas emissions.

Juliana v. United States could change all that, and for that reason both the Obama and Trump administrations have fought it with all they have. Which is why the government's lawyer, Eric Grant, argued before a three-judge panel of the Ninth Circuit Court of Appeals in December 2017 that this case would be, as Grant said, "the trial of the century." Therefore, he said, it should be stopped dead in its tracks.

In August 2015, a group of 21 young people (ages 11 to 23 as of this writing) sued President Obama, the EPA and its administrator, and a number of other federal agencies that are involved in promoting the use of fossil fuels.[34]

Each of these young people argued that they were being harmed by climate change, and that the various federal departments, by promoting the production and use of fossil fuels, were contributing to that harm.

The lawsuit's leading group noted in a summary,

> Lead plaintiff Kelsey Juliana alleges algae blooms harm the water she drinks, and low water levels caused by drought kill the wild salmon she eats.
>
> Plaintiff Xiuhtezcatl Roske-Martinez alleges increased wildfires and extreme flooding jeopardize his personal safety.
>
> Plaintiff Alexander Loznak alleges record setting temperatures harm the health of the hazelnut orchard on his

> *family farm, an important source of both revenue and food*
> *for him and his family.*
>
> *Plaintiff Jacob Lebel alleges drought conditions required*
> *his family to install an irrigation system at their farm.*[35]

If they were to win, billions of dollars a year in federal support and subsidies to the fossil-fuel industry would vanish and be replaced by a nationwide program involving all these agencies (and more) to replace fossil fuels with green alternatives.

In Nature's Trust

Unlike earlier environment-related cases, this case took a novel approach, based on a brilliant book by University of Oregon law professor Mary Christina Wood.

In *Nature's Trust: Environmental Law for a New Ecological Age*, Wood looks back over more than a thousand years of common and constitutional law and finds that one of the main reasons governments are formed is to hold what most of us would think of as "the commons" in "trust" for their citizens.

Reaching all the way back to AD 535, Wood noted, "The Institutes of Justinian declared: 'By the law of nature these things are common to mankind—the air, running water, the sea and consequently the shores of the sea.'" The doctrine protecting these commons is a core governmental function that has been at the core of virtually every nation formed since then.

Sir Matthew Hale revived the concept in medieval England, and it found its way into British common law, where it sits to this day. The idea is that one of the very foundational responsibilities of government is to protect and hold in trust for all its citizens those parts of the commons that are necessary for life and liberty.

The American basis for the doctrine is found in an 1883 Supreme Court case brought by the state of Illinois against the Illinois Central Railroad. The railroad had bought a large chunk of Lake Michigan shoreline, including the waters and the sand under the waters immediately offshore. The state challenged the claim, saying that the waters were part of the commons and couldn't be owned or despoiled by that private corporation.

Justice Stephen Field wrote for the majority, "The ownership of the navigable waters of the harbor and of the lands under them is a subject of public concern to the whole people of the state. The trust with which they are held therefore is governmental, and cannot be alienated."

Field quoted Chief Justice Roger B. Taney's 1842 decision in *Martin v. Waddell*:

> "When the Revolution took place, the people of each state became themselves sovereign, and in that character hold the absolute right to all their navigable waters and the soils under them for their own common use, subject only to the rights since surrendered by the Constitution to the general government."[36]

Field concluded,

> The soil under navigable waters being held by the people of the state in trust for the common use and as a portion of their inherent sovereignty, any act of legislation concerning their use affects the public welfare.

In the years since then, case law (including state constitutions and state laws) has included wetlands, parklands, wildlife, groundwater, and—most important—the air as part of the "trust assets" that government must hold and protect on behalf of its citizens.

Our Children's Trust

The young people bringing *Juliana v. United States* to the federal district court in Oregon (and then to the Ninth Circuit) claimed that the federal government and its agencies were specifically responsible for the harms that had and would befall the young people, because those agencies promoted the use of fossil fuels.

The plaintiffs are charging that (1) the US government is failing to protect the commons (in this case, the warming atmosphere and the acidifying oceans), and (2) the government is itself facilitating that harm.

The Justice Department attorney tried to shift the blame from the federal government, telling federal District Judge Ann Aiken, "It is really third parties that are contributing to this," he said, "not the United States."

Several of the young people who were in court that day responded.

Jacob Lebel, a 22-year-old plaintiff from Roseburg, Oregon, said,

> *I see the forest dying around my farm due to drought stress and I breathe the smoke that is getting worse every summer. To know that this is just the beginning of the*

*destabilization that climate change has in store for my
generation is one of the worst feelings I can think of. Of all
the crimes a nation's government can commit, the deliberate
and conscious poisoning of the very basic resources on
which its youngest citizens depend is the most far-reaching
and insidious.*

Jayden F., a 15-year-old plaintiff from Rayne, Louisiana, replied,

*My government continues to promote the development of
fossil fuels even though they know that it threatens my life
and my home. They opened up the Gulf of Mexico for gas
leasing, the Bayou Pipeline is going to pass through most of
South Louisiana, including my town. These actions are only
going to further climate change and worsen the storms and
flooding in my area.*

And Julia Olson, executive director and chief legal counsel of Our Children's Trust and co-counsel for youth plaintiffs, added,

*The Constitution is silent on whether there should
be a fossil fuel energy system, but it speaks loudly about
protecting liberty. We believe the courts will use their
authority under the Constitution to protect young
Americans from the climate crisis.*[37]

While hearing *Juliana* in 2018, Judge Aiken wrote that "[i]n its broadest sense, the term 'public trust' refers to the fundamental understanding that no government can legitimately abdicate its core sovereign powers."

Mirroring Professor Wood's logic, Aiken cited the Institutes of Justinian: "The following things are by natural law common to all—the air, running water, the sea, and consequently the seashore."

Aiken also agreed that this case was logically following in the footsteps of the Court's decision in *Illinois Central Railroad Co. v. Illinois*, writing, "The state can no more abdicate its trust over property in which the whole people are interested, like navigable waters and soils under them . . . than it can abdicate its police powers in the administration of government and the preservation of the peace."

She even quoted Wood's book, writing that "[t]he government, as trustee, has a fiduciary duty to protect the trust assets from damage so that current and future trust beneficiaries will be able to enjoy the benefits of the trust."

Another comment from Aiken reveals one of the biggest reasons the federal government is now throwing pretty much everything it has against this case: "Public trust claims are unique because they concern inherent attributes of sovereignty. The public trust imposes on the government an obligation to protect the rest of the trust. A defining feature of that obligation is that it cannot be legislated away."

She added that the young people's claims that the government must own up to its public trust obligations "predate the Constitution and are secured by it."

A New Hurdle to Climate Justice

During his 30-year tenure on the Supreme Court, Justice Anthony Kennedy was the pro-environment swing vote in many cases, including *Massachusetts v. EPA*.

With Brett Kavanaugh as his replacement, *Juliana* will face a decidedly anti-environment Court. In the past, Kavanaugh has ruled that federal government agencies (like the EPA) can only regulate something that is specifically mentioned in a law.

For instance, when Kavanaugh was still on the DC Circuit Court in 2017, he ruled in *Mexichem Fluor v. EPA* that the EPA could not regulate the atmosphere-destroying refrigeration chemicals known as HFCs (hydrofluorocarbons). He argued that the Clean Air Act didn't give the EPA the power to regulate HFCs because they aren't explicitly and specifically named in the law.

The Supreme Court hasn't heard a challenge to the ruling, and Kavanaugh's strict interpretation stands.

Juliana has the potential to be a landmark case, like *Brown v. Board*, *Roe v. Wade*, and *Citizens United*.

If the Supreme Court rules that the federal government has a constitutional obligation to protect the commons for future generations, it could transform the entire American energy system in a generation.

If the plaintiffs win, then federal tax incentives for fossil-fuel exploration and extraction; leases of federal lands and offshore waters for mining, fracking, and drilling; and tax breaks and subsidies of all sorts (perhaps even military) would all have to be replaced by federal incentives and programs to promote clean and renewable power.

But the Court is often biased for the wealthy and corporate interests. The next year or two will determine if that bias will stop *Juliana* from transforming the United States economy, creating a safer planet, and making the United States a leader in climate justice. The case can be followed at YouthVGov.org.

How Communities Fight Back

There are three principal ways that activists are using the law to try to slow down and even reverse the destruction of our planet by climate change.

The first is through the political process and regulation, which the Trump administration has shown us can be a thin reed, subject to the vagaries of politics. Its rollback of previous administrations' rules and regulations to reduce poisons in our air and water, and carbon dioxide and methane (and chlorofluorocarbons) in our atmosphere, shows how fragile this strategy can be without strong and clear legislation from Congress.

The second is the property rights movement, claiming that the right of people to enjoy their environment and the stability of their lives—a logical extension of property rights as envisioned by Locke and Jefferson all the way to today—is infringed on by pollution and climate change. This is largely the "public trust" doctrine that's being pursued in the *Juliana* case by the young people in Oregon.

The third is the human rights argument. This posits that the core human rights referenced in both the Declaration of Independence and the Constitution (particularly as amended by the Bill of Rights) include the right to safety and happiness, which require a stable climate and a nontoxic environment.

The Community Environmental Legal Defense Fund (CELDF) has championed this third way for years, and more than 200 local and statewide governments have jumped on the bandwagon.

They've used this argument to fight against massive hog farms and other big ag operations, against pollution from mining and oil and gas extraction (including fracking), and against other forms of environmental local cultural destruction, from toxic waste incinerators to big-box stores.

They do this by helping communities develop their own "bills of rights" that include language like that used in this resolution passed by voters in Mendocino County, California, in 2014 in response to fracking and oil drilling. They assert that the county and its citizens have, among other rights, the explicit

(a) Right to community self-government. All residents of Mendocino County possess the right to a form of governance where they live, which recognizes that all power is inherent in the people and that all free governments are founded on the people's consent. . . .

(b) Right to clean water, air, and soil. All residents, natural communities, and ecosystems in Mendocino County possess the right to water, air, and soil that is untainted by toxins, carcinogens, particulates, nucleotides, and hydrocarbons introduced into the environment through the unconventional extraction of hydrocarbons.

(c) Rights of natural communities and ecosystems. Natural communities and ecosystems possess rights to exist and flourish within Mendocino County without harm resulting from the unconventional extraction of hydrocarbons.

(d) Right to be free from chemical trespass. All residents, natural communities, and ecosystems in Mendocino County possess the right to be free from chemical trespass resulting from the unconventional extraction of hydrocarbons.

The main opposition to CELDF's work has come from corporate interests, who want to pollute or otherwise use the commons of local communities to generate profits for themselves. These corporations use the Supreme Court–invented doctrine of corporate personhood to pit their own "rights" against the rights of the citizens in these communities, and often bring millions or tens of millions of dollars to the battle.

CELDF and the communities aligned with them have not yet succeeded, as the courts consistently have sided with corporate rights and property rights over what CELDF asserts are human rights. In the process of years of education and litigation, however, CELDF and their allies have awakened and turned tens of thousands of citizens into citizen activists while teaching people about the law, human rights, and the Constitution.

And the time may come soon when CELDF's strategy will work well. That harks back to the Michigan Supreme Court, in the 1871 case of *People ex rel. Le Roy v. Hurlbut*,[38] in which one of Michigan's most famous jurists, Judge Thomas M. Cooley, wrote,

> [L]ocal government is a matter of absolute right; and the state cannot take it away. It would be the boldest mockery to speak of a city as possessing municipal liberty where the state not only shaped its government, but at discretion sent in its own agents to administer it; or to call that system one of constitutional freedom.

The idea that local and municipal governments should have what, in that day, was referred to as the right of *home rule* (called the Cooley Doctrine in American law) was very popular and, indeed, has spread around the world.

When the Indian activist Vandana Shiva visited Mendocino County to support their and CELDF's efforts to claim these local government rights, she noted, "We forget that the term 'home rule' was the term used everywhere in the world to resist empire."

In this ruling, Justice Cooley was challenging another state Supreme Court justice, John Forrest Dillon of Iowa, who in 1868 had ruled that "substate" governments in a state may engage in an activity only if the state government itself had explicitly sanctioned it.

After Cooley's challenge to "Dillon's Rule," Texas, Indiana, Iowa, and Kentucky all recognized what could essentially be called home rule powers held by local governments.

Because the Constitution doesn't explicitly reference, in any way, the power relationship between state and local governments, it's been up to the courts to determine who has primacy and who is subordinate. In this, they've largely followed the doctrine that the Constitution defines for the federal versus state relationship: that the largest and most encompassing government has power over the smaller.

The first big bite at that came in 1903 in the case of *Atkin v. Kansas*, when the Court ruled, "Municipal corporations are, in every essential, only auxiliaries of the state for the purposes of local government."

In 1907, the US Supreme Court addressed it even more specifically, quoting Dillon himself, in the case of Hunter v. Pittsburgh, and again in 1923 in *City of Trenton v. State of New Jersey* when the Court ruled, "In the absence of state constitutional provisions safeguarding it to them, municipalities have no inherent right of self-government which is beyond the legislative control of the state."

The status of local communities has been pretty much locked in by Dillon's Rule ever since, a true challenge to those who assert local rights to things like a clean environment when the state government itself has withdrawn such rights and powers from the local government.

Polluting and monopolistic corporations love Dillon's Rule.

But if CELDF and its allies prevail, there may well be change driven from the bottom up that turns this all back to the old and well-accepted notion of home rule.

How Ideologues and Partisans Seized the Court: From Nixon to Trump

When the president does it, that means that it is not illegal.

—Richard M. Nixon

After *Brown v. Board* and its subsequent supporting decisions in the 1950s, and *Roe v. Wade* in 1973, Republicans concluded that they needed to curb—or seize—the power of the Court. The easiest way to do that would be to have as many Republican presidents in the White House as possible, as each could potentially nominate new conservative justices to the Court.

In 1968, Richard Nixon stole the presidential election, scuttling President Lyndon Johnson's Vietnam peace talks and setting up four GOP appointments to the Supreme Court. In that, he set a precedent for every Republican president since: do whatever it takes to win an election, even if that means committing treason or attacking the very core of American democracy, voting, in order to control who's on the Supreme and other federal courts.

In the spring and summer of 1968, President Johnson was trying to work out a tentative peace deal between North and South Vietnam. There was one final meeting to be held in October of that year in Paris before the peace deal would be announced.

The Vietnam War had made LBJ so unpopular that senior members of his own party sat him down and told him that he couldn't successfully run for reelection. Vice President Hubert Humphrey would run instead.

Humphrey was a Midwestern New Deal Democrat. He'd served two terms representing Minnesota in the US Senate; prior to that, he'd been a political science professor, served as mayor of Minneapolis, worked in FDR's Works Progress Administration, and founded the Minnesota Democratic-Farmer-Labor (DFL) Party (which is still a major force in Minnesota politics). After JFK's assassination, LBJ became president, and he picked Humphrey as his VP; together they won in a landslide in 1964.

But by 1968, Vietnam had turned public opinion against both men, and Humphrey needed the war behind him to beat Nixon in November's election. LBJ was on the job.

But Nixon found out that Johnson had an October surprise planned—the Vietnam peace deal. If LBJ pulled it off, and particularly if he gave a lot of the credit to his vice president, Humphrey would almost certainly become the next president of the United States.[39]

Nixon sabotaged Johnson's peace plan.

Americans didn't learn about this until 50 years after LBJ's death when the LBJ Presidential Library released hundreds of tape recordings of Johnson's presidential phone calls. Among them was a series of calls between Johnson and various people discussing, explicitly, Nixon's efforts to sabotage the Vietnam peace plan.

Everett Dirksen, with his grave demeanor and deep, gravelly voice, was the most well-respected and powerful Republican in the Senate at the time. He'd already been the Senate minority leader for a decade when LBJ called him about Nixon's plot. Here's a partial transcript:

President Johnson: [S]ome of [Nixon's] folks, including some of the old China Lobby, are going to the [South] Vietnamese embassy and saying, "Please notify the President [of South Vietnam] that if he'll hold out till November the 2nd they could get a better deal."

Senator Dirksen: Uh-huh.

President Johnson: Now, I'm reading their hand, Everett. I don't want to get this in the campaign.

Senator Dirksen: That's right.

President Johnson: And they oughtn't to be doing this. This is treason.

Senator Dirksen: I know. . . . Wherever they are, I'll try to get a hold of them tonight.[40]

Dirksen was unsuccessful in stopping Nixon, and Nixon even had the gall to call LBJ and deny that he was doing what he was doing. The tapes make for grim listening.

While there are many ways our republic would probably be different today had Nixon not committed treason to get elected in 1968, the most consequential has been the Supreme Court.

Nixon got four conservative appointments: Warren E. Burger, William Rehnquist, Harry Blackmun, and, most consequentially, Lewis Powell. Nixon's vice president, Gerald Ford, appointed a fifth justice, John Paul Stevens, after Nixon resigned in 1974.

Without Nixon, Lewis Powell may never have been on the Court. Powell's enduring Court legacy will be how he helped big money take over our government as the guiding force behind the 1976 *Buckley v. Valeo* and *First National Bank of Boston v. Bellotti* cases. Followed by *Citizens United* in 2010, they essentially handed our elections over to the highest bidders.

Reagan and the Court

After Jimmy Carter defeated Jerry Ford, not a single member of the Supreme Court died or resigned until after Reagan used his own dirty tricks to win the presidency in 1980.

In the early fall of 1980, President Carter thought he had reached a deal with newly elected Iranian President Abolhassan Bani-Sadr to secure the release of 52 hostages held by radical students at the American Embassy in Tehran.

Bani-Sadr was a moderate, and as he explained in a *Christian Science Monitor* op-ed on March 5, 2013,[41] he had successfully run for president of Iran on the popular position of releasing the hostages.

President Carter was confident that with Bani-Sadr's help, he could end the hostage crisis that had been an embarrassment since it began in November 1979. But Carter underestimated what California Governor Ronald Reagan would do to win the presidency.

The Reagan campaign had surreptitiously worked out a deal with the leader of Iran's radical faction, the Ayatollah Khomeini, to keep the hostages in captivity until after the 1980 presidential election. This would humiliate Carter and hand the election to Reagan. To paraphrase LBJ, Reagan's October surprise was nothing short of treason.

Bani-Sadr wrote, "I was deposed in June 1981 as a result of a coup against me. After arriving in France, I told a BBC reporter that I had left Iran to expose the symbiotic relationship between Khomeinism and Reaganism. Ayatollah Khomeini and Ronald Reagan had organized a clandestine negotiation, later known as the 'October Surprise,' which prevented the attempts by myself and then-US President Jimmy Carter to free the hostages before the 1980 US presidential election took place."

The Reagan campaign's secret negotiations with Khomeini were successful in sabotaging Carter and Bani-Sadr's attempts to free the hostages. And, as Bani-Sadr told the *Christian Science Monitor*, "The fact that they were not released tipped the results of the [1980] election in Reagan's favor."[42]

Iran released the hostages on January 20, 1981, at the exact minute that Reagan put his hand on the Bible. The message was clear: "We kept up our part of the deal; now we expect you to start shipping us those weapons and military spare parts you promised."

Reagan's October surprise emboldened the radical forces inside Iran, and Mohammad-Ali Rajai, a hard-right favorite of Khomeini's, replaced the politically weakened Bani-Sadr in June 1981.

Reagan illegally took money from the Iranians and used that money to destabilize Nicaragua, Honduras, and El Salvador in ways that still haunt the region and recently sent waves of refugees into the United States. And he set America on a hard-right political course that destroyed much of the New Deal and gutted America's unionized middle class.

If Carter had been able to free the hostages as he and Bani-Sadr had planned, Carter likely would have won reelection. After all, he was ahead in most polls in the months leading up to the election, and most Americans at that time saw Reagan as a radical puppet for the multimillionaire class (history proved them right).

If Reagan's campaign hadn't committed treason, Antonin Scalia and Clarence Thomas, two of the most conservative justices in the Court's history, might never have been appointed to the Supreme Court. Reagan also appointed Kennedy and O'Connor, who played pivotal roles in stealing the 2000 presidential election for another Republican: George W. Bush.

If Jimmy Carter had won the election—and he was well on his way before Reagan's treason—there's little doubt that, even with Nixon's toxic appointments, the Court would have continued to uphold New Deal era programs and values, rather than attack them as it has done since Reagan won in 1980.

George H. W. Bush Avoids Prosecution

During the week of Christmas 1992, George H. W. Bush was on his way out of office. Bill Clinton had won the White House the month before, and in a few weeks he would be sworn in as president.

But Bush's biggest concern wasn't that he'd have to leave the White House to retire back to Connecticut, Maine, or Texas (where he had homes) but, rather, that he might end up in a federal prison. Because independent counsel Lawrence Walsh was closing in on him fast, and Bush's diary was a key to it all.

Walsh had been appointed independent counsel in 1986 to investigate the Iran-Contra crimes of the Reagan administration.

Did the plot start in the spring of 1980 during the Reagan–Carter election, as a way of having the Iranians hold the hostages long enough to humiliate President Carter and cost him the election? Did William Casey do it all himself as campaign manager, or, as with Nixon in 1968, did the presidential candidate or his former-CIA-chief vice-presidential candidate participate?

Or was the Iran-Contra conspiracy limited, as Reagan and Bush insisted (and Reagan confessed on TV), to later years in the Reagan presidency, in response to a hostage-taking in Lebanon? Who knew what, and when?

Walsh had zeroed in on documents that were in the possession of Reagan's former defense secretary, Caspar Weinberger, who all the evidence showed was definitely in on the deal, and Bush's diary that could corroborate it, which is why Walsh had subpoenaed it.

Weinberger was preparing to testify that Bush knew about it and even participated, and Walsh had already, based on information he'd obtained from the investigation into Weinberger, demanded that Bush turn over his diary from the campaign.

Bush was panicked. And he only had three more weeks of safety in office.

So Bush called in his attorney general, William Barr, and asked his advice.

Barr, along with Bush, was already in trouble. The iconic *New York Times* writer William Safire referred to him not as "Attorney General" but instead as "Coverup General," noting that in another scandal—having to do with Bush selling weapons of mass destruction to Saddam Hussein—Barr was already trying to cover up for Bush, himself, and his friends.

On October 19, 1992, Safire wrote of Barr's unwillingness to appoint an independent counsel to look into Iraqgate: "Why does the Coverup-General resist independent investigation? Because he knows where it may lead: to Dick Thornburgh, James Baker, Clayton Yeutter, Brent Scowcroft and himself. He vainly hopes to be able to head it off, or at least be able to use the threat of firing to negotiate a deal."[43]

Now, just short of two months later, Bush was asking Barr for advice on how to avoid another very serious charge in the Iran-Contra crimes. How, he wanted to know, could they shut down Walsh's investigation before Walsh's lawyers got their hands on Bush's diary?

In April 2001, safely distant from the swirl of DC politics, the University of Virginia's Miller Center was compiling oral presidential histories and interviewed Barr about his time as AG in the Bush White House. They brought up the issue of the Weinberger pardon and Barr's involvement in it.

Turns out, Barr was right in the middle of it.

"There were some people arguing just for [a pardon for] Weinberger, and I said, 'No, in for a penny, in for a pound,'" Barr told the interviewer. "I went over and told the President I thought he should not only pardon Caspar Weinberger, but while he was at it, he should pardon about five others."

Which is exactly what Bush did, on Christmas Eve when most Americans weren't checking the news. The holiday notwithstanding, the result was explosive.

America knew that both Reagan and Bush were up to their necks in the Iran-Contra crimes, and both could be facing prison time as a result. The independent counsel had already obtained one conviction and three guilty pleas, and two other individuals were lined up for prosecution. And Walsh was closing in fast on Bush himself.

So, when Bush shut the investigation down by pardoning not only Weinberger but also the five others involved in the crime, destroying Walsh's ability to prosecute anybody and wiping out his leverage to get Bush's diaries, the *New York Times* ran the headline all the way across four of the six columns on the front page, screaming in all caps: "BUSH PARDONS 6 IN IRAN AFFAIR, ABORTING A WEINBERGER TRIAL; PROSECUTOR ASSAILS 'COVER-UP.'"

Bill Barr had struck, saving the political life of a Republican president so that future Republican presidential nominees wouldn't suffer under the cloud of Reagan's and Bush's crimes.

The second paragraph of the *Times* story by David Johnston laid it out:

> *Mr. Weinberger was scheduled to stand trial on Jan. 5 on charges that he lied to Congress about his knowledge of the arms sales to Iran and efforts by other countries to help underwrite the Nicaraguan rebels, a case that was expected to focus on Mr. Weinberger's private notes that contain references to Mr. Bush's endorsement of the secret shipments to Iran."[44]

When a Republican president is in serious legal trouble, Bill Barr is the go-to guy.

For William Safire, it was déjà vu all over again. Four months earlier, referring to what was then called Iraqgate (wherein Bush was selling WMDs to Iraq), Safire opened an August 31, 1992, "Essay" piece titled "Justice [Department] Corrupts Justice" by writing, "U.S. Attorney General William

Barr, in rejecting the House Judiciary Committee's call for a prosecutor not beholden to the Bush Administration to investigate the crimes of Iraqgate, has taken personal charge of the cover-up."[45]

Safire accused Barr not only of rigging the cover-up but also of being one of the criminals who could be prosecuted. "Mr. Barr," wrote Safire, ". . . could face prosecution if it turns out that high Bush officials knew about Saddam Hussein's perversion of our Agriculture export guarantees to finance his war machine." He added, "They [Barr and colleagues] have a keen personal and political interest in seeing to it that the Department of Justice stays in safe, controllable Republican hands."

In August and September, Barr succeeded in blocking the appointment of an investigator or independent counsel to look into Iraqgate. In December, he helped Bush shoot down another independent counsel, Lawrence Walsh, and eliminated any risk that George H. W. Bush would be prosecuted for his Iran-Contra crimes.

Walsh, wrote Johnston for the *Times* on Christmas Eve, "plans to review a campaign diary kept by Mr. Bush." The diary would be the smoking gun that would nail Bush to the crimes.[46]

"But," noted the article, "in a single stroke, Mr. Bush swept away one conviction, three guilty pleas and two pending cases, virtually decapitating what was left of Mr. Walsh's effort, which began in 1986."

Walsh didn't take it lying down.

The *Times* report noted that "Mr. Walsh bitterly condemned the President's action, charging that 'the Iran-contra cover-up, which has continued for more than six years, has now been completed.'"

Walsh added that the diary and notes he wanted to enter into a public trial of Weinberger represented "evidence of a conspiracy among the highest ranking Reagan Administration officials to lie to Congress and the American public."

Walsh had been fighting to get those documents ever since 1986, when he was appointed and Reagan still had two years left in office. Bush's and Weinberger's refusal to turn them over, Johnston noted in the *Times* article, could have, in Walsh's words, "forestalled impeachment proceedings against President Reagan" through a pattern of "deception and obstruction."

Barr successfully helped Bush decapitate the investigation into that president's crimes, a process he'd repeat in 2019 when President Donald Trump was accused of treason and brought in Barr to clean things up.

After Reagan and Bush the elder, Bill Clinton served eight years as president and appointed Ruth Bader Ginsburg and Stephen Breyer, bringing some balance—but not a liberal majority—back to the Court.

Then came 2000.

George W. Bush and the Court

In Florida, black people are 351 percent more likely to end up with a felony conviction than white people. Consequently, Florida's white political class made it illegal for ex-felons to vote, even after they are no longer on parole. As a result, in

2000, over half a million of Florida's African Americans were permanently removed from the voting rolls (the law was changed by ballot initiative in 2018).

So, in the 2000 elections, a "flawed"-voter purge removed somewhere between 1,100 and 22,000 black Democrats from the voting rolls (depending on whether you're using the *Washington Post's* numbers or those from the BBC).

Florida Governor Jeb Bush directed Florida Secretary of State Katherine Harris to purchase a list of convicted Texas felons and to use that list to purge voters from the Florida rolls if they had identical—or even nearly identical—names. While whites have a broad diversity of names, blacks and Hispanics tend to pull from a much smaller pool of last names. The result is that this sort of merge-purge is far more likely to pick up blacks than whites.

PolitiFact noted:

> *Twenty county election supervisors decided to ignore the state's directive, because they found the data unreliable, including a Marion County elections supervisor who found her own name on the list. Leon County Supervisor of Elections Ion Sancho said he received a list of about 700 names before the 2000 election.*
>
> *"We did a check on it and could only find 30-some felons," Sancho said. "We cleared 94 percent of the list."*[47]

In May 2001, the *Los Angeles Times* did an investigation of Jeb Bush's voter purge and found that the purge could have swung the election from Gore to Bush by purging thousands of African Americans from the voter rolls. They noted that the "felon list" was 66 percent black in Miami-Dade County, and 54 percent black in Hillsborough County, where Tampa is.

The article, datelined Miami, opened thus:

> Harry Sawyer, election supervisor in Key West, was stunned when Florida officials sent him a list of 150 convicted felons to cut from county voter rolls in mid-1999.
>
> Among those named: an election employee, another worker's husband—and Sawyer's own father. None was a felon. "It was just a mess," Sawyer said.
>
> Even worse, state officials in Tallahassee ignored clear warnings about the mounting mistakes and actually loosened criteria for matching voters' names with those of felons, putting more innocent people at risk of losing their right to vote.[48]

The company hired by Bush and Harris to compile the notorious "felon list" was then called Database Technologies, and they rejected the idea that black voters were purged because of their efforts, instead blaming it on Bush and Harris.

Additionally, the governor of Texas—George W. Bush—supplied 8,000 of the "felon list" names to Database Technologies for the Florida purge, even though they were convicted felons from Texas, not Florida. But there were a lot of names like Williams (46.7 percent in the United States are black), Jackson (53 percent in the United States are black), Robinson (44.1 percent are black), and Washington (89.9 percent are black) on the list, so regardless of where they were from, when somebody with the same last name and even a *similar* first name in Florida was found, the person was purged and prevented from voting in Florida.[49]

The US Commission on Civil Rights did a detailed analysis of the Florida election and found numerous obstacles and even implied threats to minority voters.

The disenfranchisement of Florida's voters fell most harshly on the shoulders of black voters. The magnitude of the impact and dozens of examples and individual testimonials can be found in the executive summary provided by the commission to Congress.[50]

This was nothing new for the GOP, though. Back in 1980, Paul Weyrich, cofounder of the Heritage Foundation and a Christian campaign activist for Ronald Reagan, told a group of churchgoing Republican activists: "I don't want everybody to vote. Elections are not won by a majority of people. They never have been from the beginning of our country, and they are not now. As a matter of fact, our leverage in the elections, quite candidly, goes up as the voting populace goes down."[51]

After the initial 2000 vote count came in, it was unclear who won the presidential race in Florida, for a number of reasons ("butterfly ballots" and "hanging chads" cast doubt, along with other, more insidious, irregularities).

But Florida law *requires* that if an election is won or lost by a half-percentage point or less, a recount is automatic. And so the state supreme court ordered a statewide recount.

An Astroturf Resistance in Florida

To stop the recount, the Bush campaign helped organize a "protest" by "ordinary Floridians" at the more prominent offices where the recounts were going on. In the "Brooks Brothers Riot," Republican congressional staffers, Bush campaign staffers, and lobbyists—nearly all flown in from Washington, DC—raised a ruckus, demanding that the recount be stopped.

Their efforts gained enough traction that the Bush campaign sued the Gore campaign in the Supreme Court, asserting that if the recount proceeded, Bush would almost certainly lose. On December 9, the US Supreme Court stopped the recount. Reagan's appointee Antonin Scalia issued a rare opinion in the stay, echoing the Fox News talking points of the Brooks Brothers Rioters by bizarrely questioning whether the votes that would be recounted were "legal" votes.

"The counting of votes that are of questionable legality," Scalia wrote, "does in my view threaten irreparable harm to petitioner [George W. Bush], and to the country, by casting a cloud upon what he claims to be the legitimacy of his election."

The recount was stopped after the Brooks Brothers Riot, effectively handing the election to George W. Bush (who'd lost the popular vote by over half a million votes nationwide). The margin of his "victory" in Florida was 524 votes.

Five years later, the *Washington Post*'s Al Kamen looked back at the pictures of the Brooks Brothers Rioters and found that many of the "rioters" were handsomely rewarded, receiving prestigious positions ranging from White House political director (Matt Schlapp) to director of federal affairs for Koch Industries (Tom Pyle).[52]

In 2005, the *New York Times* reported how a couple of then-little-known lawyers, both Harvard Law graduates, also played an outsized role in getting the Supreme Court to stop the recount in Florida.

"We started to assemble a team of the best lawyers and in particular the best Supreme Court lawyers in the country," Ted Cruz told the *Times* reporters in a telephone interview, "and John's name naturally came near the top of the list."[53]

John was John Roberts, now Chief Justice John Roberts.

As former clerks for Chief Justice William Rehnquist, a Nixon Supreme Court nominee, both he and Cruz knew Rehnquist well enough to craft a legal argument that Rehnquist would accept as reason to block the Florida Supreme Court's recount order.

As Cheryl Gay Stolberg and David D. Kirkpatrick wrote, "Mr. Roberts edited legal briefs produced each day by the Bush team of 400 lawyers as the case was moving through the lower courts. And he played a crucial role in editing the final 50-page Supreme Court argument, prepared in just 24 hours. He also prepared moot court questions for Mr. Olson and participated in a dress rehearsal in preparation of Mr. Olson's arguments before the court, Mr. Cruz said."[54]

President George W. Bush—the former governor of Texas—gave a helpful endorsement to Cruz when he ran for the US Senate from Texas in 2012, and Bush famously nominated John Roberts as chief justice of the Supreme Court in 2005.

Bush then went on to add the man who would be the most extreme right-winger (until Neil Gorsuch) on the Court: Samuel Alito, who famously whisper-talked back to President Obama during his State of the Union Address when Obama called out the *Citizens United* case.

Finally, a full year after five Republican appointees to the Supreme Court put Bush in the Oval Office, a consortium of news organizations (including the AP, Gannett, and the *New York Times*) performed a whole-state top-to-bottom recount of the vote, using trailer trucks filled with the state's ballots brought up to New York.[55]

Even discounting about 8,000 "confused" voters, the *Washington Post* concluded, "Gore's largest margin in a statewide recount involving all ballots comes under a scenario that sought to re-create the standards established by each of the counties in their recounts. In that case, Gore emerged with 171 more votes than Bush."[56]

Gore won the election, said the *Post*.

Similarly, the *New York Times* noted,

> If all the ballots had been reviewed under any of seven single standards, and combined with the results of an examination of overvotes, Mr. Gore would have won, by a very narrow margin. . . .
>
> Using the most restrictive standard—the fully punched ballot card—5,252 new votes would have been added to the Florida total, producing a net gain of 652 votes for Mr. Gore, and a 115-vote victory margin.

All the other combinations likewise produced additional votes for Mr. Gore, giving him a slight margin over Mr. Bush, when at least two of the three coders agreed.[57]

But the votes were never counted—because five Republican-appointed Supreme Court justices overruled Florida's state supreme court (so much for states' rights), trampling democracy and awarding George W. Bush his first term as president.

Trump and the Court

Like the four Republican presidents who preceded him, Donald Trump came to power in ways that were less than clean or legal. He broke felony campaign finance laws by paying to conceal affairs with a porn star and a *Playboy* model; he welcomed support from Russia, and possibly other foreign governments to assist his election; and he benefited from a massive voter-suppression effort that spanned 30-plus states. That campaign knocked millions of people, the vast majority of them minorities or young and elderly white people in Democratic-voting areas, off the voting rolls or prevented them from voting altogether.

George W. Bush lost the popular vote by 500,000 votes nationwide, but Trump lost it by almost three million. And without massive voter suppression (in this case in Wisconsin, Michigan, and Ohio), Trump would not have won the Electoral College, either.

President Obama nominated three Supreme Court justices: Sonia Sotomayor, Elena Kagan, and Merrick Garland. But Senate Majority Leader Mitch McConnell led Republicans in an unprecedented—and anti-constitutional—move to block Garland from ever getting a Senate hearing. Garland's nomination simply expired with Obama's term.

When Trump came into office, he picked the son of Anne Gorsuch, who'd resigned in disgrace as Ronald Reagan's EPA administrator, to replace Antonin Scalia on the bench.

Trump then appointed Brett Kavanaugh, a partisan Republican who'd advised George W. Bush on the legality of torture and other questionable acts while working in the Bush White House.

Kavanaugh, who had clerked for Justice Kennedy, had also participated with John Roberts in 2000 in advising the Bush legal team about how best to argue their case before the Supreme Court to block the Florida recount.

McConnell and Senate Republicans blocked the release of Kavanaugh's papers from the Bush White House and the Florida recount, so his complicity in those events was never thoroughly aired before the Senate confirmed him to the Court in 2018.

If We'd Had Clean Elections

"If" is always a hard game to play, but this history has to cause us to wonder how different America would be if Nixon and Reagan hadn't committed treason, and Bush and Trump hadn't benefited from election fraud.

It's unlikely that Democratic presidents would have appointed justices to the Court who would have struck down parts of the Voting Rights Act, the Affordable Care Act, various environmental rules, and numerous protections for workers and organized labor.

And we might still have a Court that would move the country forward and strengthen the middle class, rather than further cement what President Jimmy Carter characterized as the current system of "oligarchy" at the cost of democracy.[58]

PART THREE

To Save the Planet, Democratize, and Modernize the Supreme Court

Today's US Supreme Court bears little resemblance to the political makeup of our nation. While that's created a crisis of legitimacy, it's a problem with available solutions.

This section explores a few of the options available for remedying our ailing judiciary. Ultimately, part 3 of this book explores how citizens can reverse Lewis Powell's coup and break the right-wing stranglehold on the Supreme Court specifically, and on our political system generally.

Article III, Section 2, of the Constitution says that the Supreme Court is, essentially, the final arbiter of all legal disputes in the United States, "with such Exceptions, and under such Regulations as the Congress shall make."

One of those regulations has covered how many justices are on the Court at any given time, a decision that the Constitution hands to Congress.

Regulating the Number of Justices
on the Court

Congress has the power to change the number of members on the Supreme Court and has done so for nakedly political reasons several times since the founding of the republic.

Through much of our history, the court was expanded along with the country itself. Judicial regions or circuits were added as the country grew. From the country's founding until 1891, each member of the Supreme Court would also spend a few months a year "riding the circuit" as the lead judge on the circuit courts.

As new states were added, they needed their own court circuits, so the number of justices on the Supreme Court grew to accommodate the new circuits. It grew to seven in 1807 and nine in 1837. It peaked at 10 in 1863, when the 10th Circuit Court was added for California.

But going all the way back to the battle between Adams and Jefferson in 1800, Congress also had a history of "regulating" the number of justices on the Court for purely political purposes.

When the first Judiciary Act became law in 1789, it established the Supreme Court at six members.

The Federalists lost executive and legislative power in the election of 1800, but Adams wasn't about to hand over the federal government to Jefferson completely.

In the months before they had to leave, the furious Federalists passed a law reducing the size of the Court to five members, so that even if someone died or left, Jefferson would not be able to make his own appointments. Weeks after the new Democratic Republican (now known as the Democratic Party) Congress was sworn in, they undid the law, so it never had any impact.

Four generations later, for the 1864 election, Abraham Lincoln replaced his first-term VP, Maine's Hannibal Hamlin, with a Southerner and a slave owner, Andrew Johnson. Johnson had bought his first slave, a 14-year-old girl named Dolly, the same year he was elected to the Tennessee House of Representatives; over the years between then and 1865 she had borne him three children, and he'd added more slaves to his collection.

When Lincoln was assassinated in the year after he was reelected, the pro-slavery Democrat Johnson became president and things started to come apart. The culmination of that was the successful 1867 impeachment of Johnson in the House, and the Senate's inability to convict and remove him from office by a single vote.

In 1865, Supreme Court Justice John Catron died, leaving a vacancy on the Court. Catron was a slave owner, and Johnson moved to replace him with Attorney General appointee Henry Stanbery—a political friend of Johnson's.

Stanbery had been a Democrat, but he'd grown up in Pennsylvania and Ohio, so he wasn't a slaveholder or a Southerner. Nonetheless, his close affiliation with Johnson upset the Republicans who controlled Congress. He also supported Johnson's policies of pulling troops out of the South, which would have effectively ended Reconstruction in the South. Republicans in Congress were enraged at the prospect.

So, in the spirit of the Congress of 1800, Congress passed a law in July 1866 to gradually reduce the size of the Court (as individuals died or retired) from 10 members to seven. This not only blocked Johnson from appointing Stanbery but also made it unlikely that he'd get any appointments as president.

In 1868, anti-slavery Republican Ulysses S. Grant took the White House and a solid Republican majority took Congress. Johnson was no longer a threat, and Congress reregulated the Court with the Judiciary Act of 1869, which raised the number of justices to nine. It's stayed there ever since.

Congress has twice altered the number of justices on the Supreme Court, just to thwart a sitting or incoming president.

It's time to do it again.

Term Limits

Another solution to an out-of-touch Supreme Court is to increase the frequency of the Court's turnover and to make sure that every president can appoint at least two justices.

An 18-year term limit, rolled out over staggered alternate years, would accomplish both goals.

The Constitution, speaking of how long federal judges will serve, says, "The judges, both of the supreme and inferior courts, shall hold their offices during good behaviour, and shall, at stated times, receive for their services, a compensation, which shall not be diminished during their continuance in office."

The argument against Supreme Court term limits is that the only reason the Constitution specifies for removing a judge is his or her failure to engage in "good behaviour" (like other federal officials, they can also be impeached). In other words, as long as they don't misbehave, they're in for life.

But the sentence about judicial terms lumps together both Supreme Court justices and other federal judges. According to multiple constitutional scholars, that means it's possible to move judges between courts without disrupting their lifetime jobs.

This is what happens when elevating judges from the federal courts to the Supreme Court; why not the reverse?

In the *Federalist*, no. 79, Hamilton lumps the two together when referencing compensation: "The plan of the convention accordingly has provided that the judges of the United States 'shall at STATED TIMES receive for their services a compensation which shall not be DIMINISHED during their continuance in office.'"

He also noted that the sole technique for complete removal from either federal bench is impeachment: "They are liable to be impeached for malconduct by the House of Representatives, and tried by the Senate; and, if convicted, may be dismissed from office, and disqualified for holding any other. This is the only provision on the point."

In the *Federalist*, no. 78, Hamilton again conflated the types of judges when arguing for lifetime tenure: "The standard of good behavior for the continuance in office of the judicial magistracy, is certainly one of the most valuable of the modern improvements in the practice of government."

Ironically, the Supreme Court itself could determine the constitutionality of judicial term limits. Or must the justices recuse themselves? Here, the knot gets tighter and more complex; there are no easy answers, as the issue has never been subjected to legislative, executive, or judicial review.

But as Thomas Jefferson wrote to John Taylor in 1798 about the bizarre presidency of conservative John Adams: "A little patience, and we shall see the reign of witches pass over, their spells dissolve, and the people, recovering their true sight, restore their government to its true principles."[1]

The American people want the Court to be an impartial body, providing balance to the legislative and executive branches. Term-limiting Supreme Court appointments, guaranteeing every president at least two appointments, is one tool available to balance the Court.

Cameras in the Courtroom

The Supreme Court is regulated only by Congress and itself. And because Congress has largely chosen not to regulate the Court, it's chosen to give almost zero oversight to itself.

Several members of the Court don't even seem to care about the *appearance* of impropriety: Antonin Scalia went hunting with Dick Cheney weeks before deciding a case in Cheney's favor;[2] Clarence Thomas has shown up at Koch brothers events while ruling on case after case brought to the Court by Koch front groups (all while his wife indirectly takes money from the Kochs via the Heritage Foundation).[3]

The Court has likewise far removed itself from any oversight by we the people. The Court doesn't even allow Americans to remotely see Court proceedings. No cameras or recording devices whatsoever are allowed in the Court when it's in session, and they only release written transcripts after roughly a week has passed.

The benefits are obvious: civic engagement and enlightenment. The costs that have traditionally been posited are the possibility of turning a courtroom into a "circus" and the potential for witness or juror intimidation. There's also the concern that people who are ultimately found not guilty in a courtroom may be portrayed as guilty simply because they were broadcast as a defendant in court.

The Federal Rules of Civil Procedure—which Congress passed at the request of the Supreme Court in 1937—broadly govern what's allowed and not allowed in a courtroom. They were designed "to secure the just, speedy, and inexpensive determination of every action and proceeding."

In 1953, the rules added, "Except as otherwise provided by a statute or these rules, the court must not permit the taking of photographs in the courtroom during judicial proceedings or the broadcasting of judicial proceedings from the courtroom."

In the 1990s, the Second and Ninth Circuit Courts experimented with permitting television recording of courtroom activity. After all, there are generally no witnesses, and never a jury to be intimidated, and the defendants rarely appear in person in these courts.

The experiment was successful, and the Ninth Circuit has continued to record its proceedings.

The Supreme Court has no jury (arguably, it is the jury) and no defendants (in the cinematic sense). There's really no good justification for it to prevent video or audio recordings, particularly now that cameras can be made so small as to be functionally invisible to the justices and the lawyers pleading before them.

Article III, Section 2, of the Constitution gives Congress the power, with a simple majority, to "regulate" the Supreme Court. A great starting point would be a simple law requiring the Court to allow nonintrusive live audio/video streaming and recording of its public sessions.

The Constitutional Amendment Remedy for an Out-of-Control Court

The Court has overruled itself 125 times in its history, usually after much time had passed and public sentiment changed, or because new appointments to the Court caused an ideological shift on the bench itself.[4]

The Court has also been overruled by Congress passing new (and sometimes clarifying) laws 59 times, in areas widely ranging from tax law to immigration to education and crime.[5]

But when the Court uses judicial review to overturn laws, and then holds fast to that conclusion over a substantial period of time, the only remedy that Congress and we the people have is to modify our founding document itself.

Out of more than 24,000 attempts, Congress has successfully amended the Constitution only 18 times in our nation's history (the first time for all 10 amendments in the Bill of Rights). In six of those instances, Congress (representing we the people) used the amendment process to directly "overthrow" the will of the Court.[6]

The process of amending the Constitution can be drawn out, and even bloody. The 27th Amendment, for example, was first introduced to Congress in 1791 but not ratified until

1992. The 13th, 14th, and 15th Amendments wouldn't exist if thousands of Americans hadn't died fighting to secure those rights.

The Equal Rights Amendment, introduced in 1972, is still three states short of ratification.[7] This, for a single-sentence Amendment that simply says, "Equality of rights under the law shall not be denied or abridged by the United States or by any state on account of sex," which is strongly supported by an overwhelming majority of Americans.

When the public sentiment is strong, though, Congress and the states can move fast. For example, the 26th Amendment lowered the voting age to 18. It was first introduced in Congress on March 10, 1971, and ratified just four months later on July 1: a record for the process.

FDR first proposed lowering the voting age during World War II, and Georgia lowered its voting age to 18 in 1943. Eisenhower called for it in his State of the Union address in 1954, and Richard Nixon endorsed it too. But those of us who remember the era give a lot of the credit to Barry McGuire's song "Eve of Destruction," with its haunting lyric "You're old enough to kill, but not for voting."

Released in 1965, the song quickly hit the Billboard Top 100, and when I was working as a DJ in 1969 and 1970, it was one of the most frequently requested and played of the hourly "golden oldies." It helped galvanize a movement that crested in the spring of 1971.

While there's no big hit song today complaining about how the Supreme Court simply invented the twin doctrines of *corporate personhood* and *money is free speech*—the central doctrines that have led us to such a corrupted political system—there is a broad and substantial movement across the nation to amend the Constitution to roll back both.[8]

Amending the Constitution can be a glacially slow process, but it is nonetheless an important way for we the people, via Congress and the states, to remedy harms wrought by the Court.

The Last Resort: Strip the Courts

The year 1981 was a big one for court-stripping—or, as it's sometimes called, jurisdiction-stripping. No fewer than 30 pieces of legislation were introduced into the US House of Representatives by Republican congressmen that included court-stripping provisions. It was a huge topic of discussion and legal activity among Republicans.

And a young lawyer working in Ronald Reagan's Justice Department, an up-and-comer named John Roberts, was hot on the trail.

Court-stripping is based on the idea that Congress has the power, under the Constitution, to pass laws that include provisions that specifically prevent (or strip the jurisdiction of) the Supreme Court (or any other federal court, if stipulated) from ruling on that particular law or issue's constitutionality.

It's based on Article III, Section 2, of the Constitution, which says, "[T]he supreme [sic] Court shall have appellate Jurisdiction, both as to Law and Fact, with such Exceptions, and under such Regulations as the Congress shall make."

In 1954, the Supreme Court ruled, in *Brown v. Board*, that the mostly Southern states that were segregated had to integrate their schools. Virginia shut down its entire state school system for a year in defiance; other states opened private all-white "segregation academies" such as the one that Mississippi Senator Cindy Hyde-Smith famously went to and sent her daughter to.

Brown provoked a mini industry among right-wing white racists: Fred Koch's beloved John Birch Society was putting up "Impeach Earl Warren" billboards across the nation and publishing articles and pamphlets tying civil rights activists to communism; hundreds of all-white private schools opened; and conservative scholars of the Supreme Court and the Constitution searched through old books and debates from the founding era to that day looking for rationales to overturn the decision.

Other than years of disruption to public education and a redoubled effort by conservatives to keep public schools funded with local property taxes (so that poor and/or black schools would continue to turn out poorly educated students), not a great deal came of the opposition to *Brown v. Board.*

But defying the Court became a much bigger business in 1973, when the Court in *Roe v. Wade* ruled that women have the right, at least in the first trimester of a pregnancy, to choose to have an abortion pretty much anywhere in the country, for any reason.

The Catholic Church was the first to react with outrage, but the generally anti-Catholic Protestant churches initially supported a woman's right to choose an abortion.

In 1979, for example, the Baptist Joint Committee went to federal court to oppose the Hyde Amendment, which banned federal monies from paying for abortions; the Baptists' rationale was that if the federal government forbade federal money from being used for abortions, then the US government had, essentially, adopted Catholic doctrine, and thus violated the Establishment Clause of the Constitution. In other words, the Baptists, who in 1979 supported a woman's right to an abortion, saw the Catholic opposition to abortion and Catholic-promoted anti-abortion legislation as an attempt to influence our government that was so severe, they said it violated the part of the Constitution that says the government shall not establish a state religion.

But just a year later, the leaders of some of the most powerful and prominent white evangelical Protestant churches realized that opposing abortion could be a religious and political/financial marketing and expansion opportunity of huge proportions.

The Southern Baptist movement in the United States, like many of the Protestant churches, was heavily invested in white supremacy. Founded in 1845, the Southern Baptists had supported segregation and Jim Crow laws for over a century, and even in 2012, their chief lobbyist, Richard Land, said on his radio show that white people seeing young black men as "threatening" was "understandable," because they are "statistically more likely to do you harm than a white man."

But that was just the warm-up. Land went on to call Al Sharpton and Jesse Jackson "racial ambulance chasers" and "race mongers." His comments caused a stir, and the denomination formally reprimanded him, but he wasn't fired.[9] Just a generation earlier, such sentiments could have been heard from the pulpit.

The deep white supremacist roots of the anti-abortion movement combined nicely with white racial outrage over

Brown to form the perfect political issue for men like Jerry Falwell.

The original anti-abortion movement started just before the Civil War, when in 1858 the American Medical Association (AMA) launched a movement to criminalize abortion among white women and place the occasional medically necessary abortion procedure exclusively in the hands of doctors.

In this, the AMA—which was entirely made up of white men at the time, and probably even 100 percent Protestant—was part of a WASP male structure in America that saw their power endangered by a growing population (largely through immigration) of "nonwhite" people, combined with a threat to male control from a growing women's suffrage movement.

As researchers Nicola Beisel and Tamara Kay wrote for a 2004 paper published in the *American Sociological Review*, "[T]he nineteenth-century politics of abortion were simultaneously racial and gender politics. Claims that physicians played on fears of independent women miss what was at stake: Anglo-Saxon control of the state and dominance of society."[10]

Doing a deep dive into the publications, literature, and history of the anti-abortion movement in the late 19th and early 20th centuries, they found, "While laws regulating abortion would ultimately affect all women, physicians argued that middle-class, Anglo-Saxon married women were those obtaining abortions, and that their use of abortion to curtail childbearing threatened the Anglo-Saxon race."

Noting that the "white race" in that era was so tightly defined that it didn't include Jews or Catholics, and even explicitly defined Celts (mostly Catholic Irish) and Teutons (mostly

Germans, many of them Catholic) as other than "white," and that more than 500,000 "white" men of Anglo-Saxon ancestry had died in the Civil War, giving an instant boost to nonwhite populations, the AMA and their white supremacist allies succeeded by the 1890s in putting into place laws that forbade abortion in virtually every state. The laws were largely ignored in "nonwhite" communities but were rigorously enforced against "white" women.

Beisel and Kay wrote,

> Anglo-Saxon political control in northern cities and states depended on numerical dominance at the polls, which led to concerns about the reproductive prowess of Anglo-Saxon women. In other words, reproduction of an aspect of the racial structure—political dominance—was tied to ... women's role as mothers.

The racist history of the anti-abortion movement wasn't lost on Jerry Falwell, who had spent decades since *Brown v. Board* opening, running, and authorizing whites-only "Christian" private schools.

One of the most prolific multimillionaire marketers among the evangelical Protestant community, Falwell seems to have realized that being opposed to abortion could be a huge fundraiser and publicity machine for his growing televangelism business. As a bonus, it dovetailed nicely with the white supremacist philosophy that animated his all-white school empire.

Merging the two needed a bit of marketing, though, and they needed a high-profile politician to bring this to a national stage. The candidacy of Ronald Reagan in 1980 was their opportunity to make serious political hay.

At the same time, the conservative heavyweight and cofounder of the Heritage Foundation and ALEC, Paul Weyrich, who famously said, "I don't want everyone to vote," had been arguing for over a year that merging "local control" of schools to keep them all-white with an anti-abortion message, presumably to keep the white race growing, only made sense for the Republican Party and the conservative movement.

Initially, the problem was that Reagan, as California governor, had supported and signed a bill that legalized and made abortion widely available. His vice-presidential running mate, George H. W. Bush, was an ardent and outspoken supporter of Planned Parenthood.

But Falwell, Weyrich, and others prevailed on Reagan, and when he ran for president in 1980, he flipped positions to support a constitutional amendment to ban abortion nationwide. Bush quietly followed.

Falwell then led a movement of white evangelical preachers (particularly those with a high TV profile) to support Reagan, and, as Steven P. Miller wrote for *Salon* in 2014, "That year [1980] witnessed a conclusive pivot in modern evangelical politics—a pivot, indeed, in the image of American evangelicalism as a whole."

Referring to Falwell as, by 1979, a political consultant as well as a religious leader, Miller noted, "During the 1980 campaign, Ronald Reagan and the evangelical conservatives engaged in a very public courting ritual."[11]

Reagan, of course, had kicked off his 1980 presidential campaign with a speech about education and states' rights to an all-white crowd near Philadelphia, Mississippi, where three civil rights activists had been murdered just years before. Willing to say and do whatever it took to take the White House, Reagan was the perfect vessel for a white supremacy message opposing forced integration, welfare for black people, and abortion for white women.

Thus, after Reagan's installation in the White House in January 1981, his Justice Department was hard at work, both on an anti-abortion constitutional amendment (a long shot— more than 24,000 have been submitted to Congress, and only 27 have ever made it through the process to become part of the Constitution) and on a frenetic search for other ways to satisfy an explosively growing anti-abortion movement that was daily being jacked into hysteria by Falwell and his supporters (a process that, within a decade, would lead to the first murder of an abortion doctor in the United States).

The Roberts Plan to Strip the Courts

Reagan's administration brought together a constellation of conservative white men to change the face of America. Ted Olson, who later argued *Bush v. Gore* before the US Supreme Court, led the Justice Department's Office of Legal Counsel. As an assistant attorney general, Olson worked with counselor to the attorney general Ken Starr (appointed to that job in 1981), who was later (1989–1993) George H. W. Bush's solicitor general. Other new faces Reagan hired included Samuel Alito and John Roberts.

Starr tasked Roberts, a staunchly anti-abortion Catholic, with reviewing the entire history of the US Supreme Court for cases that suggested a legislative or administrative way to overturn *Roe v. Wade* and possibly even *Brown v. Board*.

Roberts wrote an extraordinary 27-page document that's almost unknown, in the form of a memo on the letterhead of the Office of the Attorney General to Ken Starr, signed by Roberts as special assistant to the attorney general. It is titled, "Proposals to Divest the Supreme Court of Appellate Jurisdiction: An Analysis in Light of Recent Developments." (The memo starts on page 66 of the online archive cited.)[12]

Roberts wrote that he had found "over twenty bills [pending in Congress] which would divest the Supreme Court (and, in most instances, lower federal courts as well) of jurisdiction to hear certain types of controversies, ranging from school prayer and desegregation cases to abortion cases."

What Roberts and his researchers found was substantial.

Court-stripping is based on the Exceptions Clause of Article III, Section 2, of the Constitution, which stipulates that the courts exist *"with such Exceptions, and under such Regulations as the Congress shall make."*

Roberts noted eagerly in his memo that "the exceptions clause by its terms contains no limit…. This clear and unequivocal language is the strongest argument in favor of congressional power and the inevitable stumbling block for those would read the clause in a more restricted fashion."

Roberts was looking at the nuclear option. If he could build a strong case for Congress passing a law against abortion (or against desegregation), and persuade Congress to use the Exceptions Clause to render the courts moot, then this could be the magic bullet to restore segregation and recriminalize abortion!

Roberts concluded with a 1968 comment from Sam Ervin of North Carolina, one of the Senate's most outspoken opponents of racial integration and abortion.

He wrote, "As Senator Ervin noted during hearings on the exceptions clause, 'I don't believe that the Founding Fathers could have found any simpler words or plainer words in the English language to say what they said, which is that the appellate jurisdiction of the Supreme Court is dependent entirely upon the will of Congress.'"

Roberts agreed: "[W]e are not considering a constitutional clause that is by its nature indeterminate and incapable of precise or fixed meaning, such as the due process clause or the prohibition on unreasonable searches and seizures."

This was clearly the original intent, Roberts argued, because "the exceptions clause 'was not debated' by the Committee of Detail which drafted it, or the whole Convention."[13]

Citing the *Federalist*, no. 81, Roberts wrote, "Hamilton noted that the clause would enable 'the government to modify [appellate jurisdiction] in such a manner as will best answer the ends of public justice and security,' and that appellate jurisdiction was 'subject to any exceptions and regulations which may be thought advisable.'"[14]

Section III of Roberts's screed on court-stripping dives deep into Supreme Court decisions to find rulings explicitly saying that Congress can regulate the Supreme Court and block the Court from ruling on particular issues.

Beginning with the 1869 decision *Ex parte McCardle*, Roberts wrote, "A unanimous Court upheld the power of Congress to divest the Supreme Court of jurisdiction. The Court clearly based its decision on Congress' power under the exceptions clause. Chief Justice Chase began the opinion by recognizing that the appellate jurisdiction of the Court "is conferred 'with such exceptions and under such regulations as Congress shall make.'"

Quoting Chase again, Roberts added his own emphasis: "We are not at liberty to inquire into the motives of the legislature. We can only examine into its power under the Constitution; *and the power to make exceptions to the appellate jurisdiction of this Court is given by express words* [emphasis Roberts's]."

He continued his historical exposé of court-stripping with another 1869 decision, *Ex parte Yerger*, and then *United States v. Klein* (1872), *Wiscart v. Dauchy* (1796), *Durousseau v. United States* (1810), *Daniels v. Railroad* (1865), and *The Francis Wright* (1881).

In *The Francis Wright*, Roberts found that Chief Justice Morrison R. Waite (whose Court oversaw the infamous 1886 "corporate personhood" *Santa Clara County v. Southern Pacific Railroad* case) wrote for a unanimous Court, quoting him as follows: "Not only may whole classes of cases be kept out of the jurisdiction altogether, but particular classes of questions may be subjected to re-examination and review, while others are not."[15]

Each case strengthened the idea that Congress could simply pass a law, without even needing a supermajority, that barred the Supreme Court from ruling on a set of issues—like Reagan's hot-button issues of school desegregation and abortion.

Moving toward late-19th-century decisions, Roberts quoted the Court in *Colorado Central Consolidated Mining Co. v. Turck*

(1893): "[I]t has been held in an uninterrupted series of decisions that this Court exercises appellate jurisdiction only in accordance with the acts of Congress upon the subject."

Roberts, in his own voice, added, "Again, it bears emphasis that the basis for this theory is the implicit exercise by Congress of its exceptions power when it makes a limited grant of jurisdiction."

Court-Stripping in the 20th Century

Still building his case, Roberts jumped into 20th-century rulings, starting with *National Mutual Insurance Co. v. Tidewater Transfer Co.* (1948). Writing for the majority, Justice Felix Frankfurter noted in the decision, "Congress need not give this Court any appellate power; it may withdraw appellate jurisdiction once conferred and it may do so even while a case is sub judice."[16]

About the 1944 *Yakus v. United States* case, Roberts wrote, "Justice Rutledge noted . . . that 'Congress has plenary power to confer or withhold jurisdiction.'"

Regarding *Flast v. Cohen* (1968), Roberts quoted from Justice William O. Douglas, who wrote, "[A]s respects our appellate jurisdiction, Congress may largely fashion it as Congress desires by reason of the express provisions of Section 2, Article III. *See Ex parte McCardle.*"

In Section IV of his memo, Roberts again went back to the framing of the Constitution and brought us up to the present day, quoting another dozen or so cases that referenced, less directly, the power of Congress to exempt the Court from certain issues or decisions.

Roberts also noted that the original Judiciary Act (which created the federal court system) also refers to Congress's power of exception.

Roberts and many of his colleagues in the Reagan administration and the Republicans in Congress believed that if school desegregation and legalized abortion stood, their (and their base voters') white male power was in real danger of being diminished. It was an existential emergency to them, as much as a political opportunity.

In the face of such an emergency, they seriously considered—and tried more than 30 times that year in Congress—a nuclear option that had never been used in a big way before: court-stripping.

A Planetary Emergency

In retrospect, the energy and concern of Roberts and his colleagues seem almost quaint.

Now, the Supreme Court has a solid majority of men who support both white male supremacy (remember that Thomas even supported gutting the Voting Rights Act) and the criminalization of abortion. But, unlike Roberts's early days and the abortion/desegregation issues, today the United States and the world are facing an existential emergency.

Global warming and the atmospheric carbon that cause it have reached the point where it's causing massive death of nonhuman species across the planet[17] and producing such severe weather (both droughts and floods) that the costs today are in the hundreds of billions across the United States and in the trillions worldwide.[18]

Deserts are swallowing farmlands, driving refugee crises from the Middle East (the Arab Spring was touched off by an explosion in wheat prices), and many of the refugees from Central America trying to make it into the United States are similarly fleeing destabilized areas where crops are failing.

Every mass extinction in the history of the planet has been caused by climate change. In four of the five previous mass extinctions, the climate change was caused by volcanic activity throwing massive amounts of greenhouse gases into the atmosphere (and possibly the fifth, although it may also have purely been due to a meteorite hitting Earth); and in each case, warming past 5 to 7 degrees Celsius was enough to wipe out 70 to 95 percent of all life on Earth.

Our civilization itself is already teetering in part because of global warming; the extinction of humanity could follow if something is not done immediately.

Yet fossil-fuel billionaires not only have captured control of the entire Republican Party but also appear to have control over most of the Supreme Court.

Court-stripping is the ultimate nuclear option. Although former Senate Majority Leader Harry Reid agonized for years before partially blowing up the filibuster, that was peanuts compared with court-stripping.

If a Democratic-majority Congress were to pass a law forbidding the Supreme Court from ruling on issues of, for example, money in politics or regulation of greenhouse gases, then when Republicans regained control, they'd almost certainly pass laws reversing those actions.

Likewise, Republicans could take the power of court-stripping even further, perhaps damaging our democratic republic in ways from which it would never recover.

Thus, court-stripping should be used only in the case of a truly existential emergency.

But, should the nation reach the point where all other options have been tried and failed, and we're looking at the possible failure of our civilization or humanity, it's a good weapon to have in what FDR called the "arsenal of democracy."

Taking Democracy Back from the Court

Just a few hundred years before the American Revolution, many countries, from Europe to China, had legal policies forcing commoners to be tortured before their testimony in court could be considered legal and credible. Average people had no rights, and the king and the elite owned literally everything.

If one were to imagine power and wealth as a pyramid, the top 1 percent were at the very top, and power and wealth decreased as the pyramid got wider, representing more and more people. The vast mass of people were broke or in debt, and powerless.

The American Revolution kicked off with a rebellion against the monopolistic East India Company at the Boston Tea Party, and it sought to flip that pyramid upside down, putting most of the power in the hands of we the people through elected representatives, with the stabilizing and corrective authority of the executive and judicial branches of government.

In 1971, Lewis Powell advised the captains of industry and inherited wealth to reach out and take over the institutions of governance as well as the institutions of social control, including the media and education. Following the lead of Powell, that outreach included seizing control of the Supreme Court itself.

To control the Court, they needed their acolytes to occupy the White House, regardless of what it took to put them there. But even with explicit treason in 1968 (and Ford's benefit from it) and something that may well have been treason in 1980, Republican presidents were only able to put people on the Court who they hoped would reliably rule on the side of their donor class. It often didn't work out that way, as the GOP saw, to their frustration, with Republican-appointed justices such as David Souter and Anthony Kennedy.

In part to solve this problem, the donor class, led by a small group of petrobillionaires and their friends, helped fund the Federalist Society, which reached out to law students; found the most reliably conservative among them; and groomed them for future positions on federal courts, including the Supreme Court itself.

In service of great wealth and corporate power, the Court, particularly since the Reagan years, has exacerbated both wealth inequality and poverty among the working class in the United States. These new dynamics are leading to social, cultural, and political instability—crises that Donald Trump exploited in his campaign in 2016.

With the George W. Bush presidency, the American Bar Association's ratings—previously the gold standard for judges and Supreme Court justices—were diminished in favor of ratings from the Federalist Society. With the Trump administration, the ABA was totally marginalized, and only justices put forward by the billionaire-funded Society were even considered for the Supreme Court.

By putting corporate and property rights over human and voting rights, the Supreme Court has devastated the right to unionize in the United States, destroying what little political and economic power the middle class acquired during the New Deal era of 1933–81.

The Court deprived American workers of their ability to sue employers and forced those with employment contracts out of the courts and into corporate-run privatized "courts" conducting what's known as *binding arbitration*.

Simultaneously, the Court made it harder for poor, young, and elderly white people to vote, and struck down a wide range of voting protections for people of color.

These events together have eroded democracy in the United States and elevated the very wealthy to positions of economic and political power not seen since the Gilded Age.

They would be *troubling* for the nature and future of democracy and the ability of the working and middle classes to reclaim any of the gains they made during the New Deal era.

This is a *problem* when you're trying to get out of a depression as FDR did, and it took him five years to persuade the Court—through threats and entreaties—to back down.

But with climate change now representing an existential threat to the future of civilization itself, and the Court occupied by justices who have (through their actions, rulings, and associations) professed fealty to the power of fossil-fuel billionaires and polluting industries, this has become a crisis that requires a serious plan of action.

Therefore, Americans must now consider ways to diminish the power of the Supreme Court, work around it, or pack it as FDR proposed. And, fortunately, the Constitution itself offers several ways to accomplish that, as outlined in this book.

The question now is whether members of the political class—principally the Democratic Party—will have the courage and ability to take on the Court and restore democratic economic and political power to We the People. Are we ready?

The future of the world may depend on it.

NOTES

Introduction

1. https://www.nytimes.com/2019/03/05/opinion/oppression-majority
   .html
2. https://www.politico.com/story/2019/02/04/democrats-taxes-economy-
   policy-2020-1144874
3. https://today.yougov.com/topics/politics/articles-reports/2015/02/08/
   majority-support-requiring-paid-leave
4. https://thehill.com/policy/technology/364528-poll-83-percent-of-voters-
   support-keeping-fccs-net-neutrality-rules
5. http://www.pewresearch.org/fact-tank/2018/03/27/americans-
   complicated-feelings-about-social-media-in-an-era-of-privacy-concerns/
6. https://www.kff.org/health-costs/press-release/poll-majorities-of-
   democrats-republicans-and-independents-support-actions-to-lower-drug-
   costs-including-allowing-americans-to-buy-drugs-from-canada/
7. John Locke, *Two Treatises on Government*, Chapter 2, "State of Nature,"
   1689.
8. Locke, *Two Treatises on Government*.
9. Armen Alchian and Harold Demsetz, "The Property Right Paradigm,"
   Journal of Economic History 33, no. 1 (1973): 16–27.
10. https://phys.org/news/2017-09-mathematics-sixth-mass-extinction.html
11. https://theintercept.com/2015/07/30/jimmy-carter-u-s-oligarchy-
    unlimited-political-bribery/

Part One

1. The divine right posits that a god has chosen the king or queen, and that
   person rules by the will of that god. As of this writing, for example, the
   title of the current queen of England, Elizabeth II, is "Elizabeth II, *by
   the Grace of God*, of the United Kingdom of Great Britain and Northern
   Ireland and of her other realms and territories Queen, Head of the
   Commonwealth, Defender of the Faith."
2. Published in 1748.
3. https://founders.archives.gov/documents/Franklin/01-04-02-0037
4. http://press-pubs.uchicago.edu/founders/documents/a1_8_18s16
   .html
5. https://scholar.princeton.edu/sites/default/files/Judicial_Review_Civil_
   War_0.pdf
6. https://www.virginia.edu/woodson/courses/aas-hius366a/lincoln.html
7. https://www.reuters.com/article/usa-tax/three-quarters-of-americans-
   favor-higher-taxes-for-wealthy-reuters-ipsos-poll-idUSL2N1MM024

8. https://www.reuters.com/investigates/special-report/usa-election-progressives/

9. https://static1.squarespace.com/static/5aa9be92f8370a24714de593/t/5acba4a02b6a289d08e62559/1523295392739/JD_Report_Final_040918_LR.pdf

10. https://www.reuters.com/investigates/special-report/usa-election-progressives/

11. https://thinkprogress.org/pro-choice-america-majority-d8963029ae45/

12. https://www.prnewswire.com/news-releases/breaking-americansby-94---overwhelmingly-support-the-equal-rights-amendment-era-300286472.html

13. http://www.pewresearch.org/fact-tank/2016/12/14/most-americans-favor-stricter-environmental-laws-and-regulations/

14. The Court restricted prisoners' rights in *Minneci v. Pollard*.

15. The Court allowed Southern states to restrict black voters' rights in *Shelby County v. Holder*.

16. https://www.nytimes.com/2013/06/26/us/supreme-court-ruling.html

17. The Court restricted workers' right to sue in *Epic Systems Corp. v. Lewis*.

18. A facsimile is shown here: https://scholarlycommons.law.wlu.edu/cgi/viewcontent.cgi?article=1000&context=powellmemo.

19. http://jfk.hood.edu/Collection/Weisberg%20Subject%20Index%20Files/P%20Disk/Powell%20Lewis%20F/Item%2028.pdf

20. The full text of the Powell Memo is found at http://reclaimdemocracy.org/powell_memo_lewis/.

21. https://www.law.cornell.edu/supremecourt/text/425/748

22. https://www.bradleyfdn.org/prizes/winners/the-federalist-society

23. *Connecticut General Life Insurance Co. v. Johnson*, 303 U.S. 77 (1938), https://supreme.justia.com/cases/federal/us/303/77/.

24. https://www.heritage.org/the-constitution/report/the-originalism-revolution-turns-30-evaluating-its-impact-and-future

25. https://caselaw.findlaw.com/us-supreme-court/433/36.html

26. https://www.firstthings.com/article/1996/11/the-end-of-democracy-our-judicial-oligarchy

27. https://www.realclearpolitics.com/2012/07/29/interview_with_supreme_court_justice_antonin_scalia_286094.html

28. https://www.law.cornell.edu/supct/html/07-290.ZO.html

29. Dumas Malone, *Jefferson and His Time*, 6 vols. (Boston: Little, Brown & Co., 1981).

30. Jefferson starts out the letter pleading with Kercheval to keep his comments to himself; Kercheval's failure to do so is probably why there are not more of these kinds of rants from Jefferson or the other founders to be easily found. He further points out that the United States was the first republic in millennia; and so, of course, many mistakes were made in drafting first the Articles of Confederation and then the Constitution.

31. http://www.historyofwar.org/sources/acw/grant/chapter16d.html

32. Letter to Samuel Kercheval, July 12, 1816.

33. The *Federalist*, no. 57, http://constitution.org/fed/federa57.htm.

34. Martin Gilens and Benjamin I. Page, "Testing Theories of American Politics: Elites, Interest Groups, and Average Citizens," *Perspectives on Politics* 12, no. 3 (2014): 564–581, https://www.cambridge.org/core/journals/perspectives-on-politics/article/testing-theories-of-american-politics-elites-interest-groups-and-average-citizens/62327F513959D0A30 4D4893B382B992B.

35. Martin Gilens and Benjamin I. Page, "Critics argued with our analysis of U.S. political inequality. Here are 5 ways they're wrong," *Washington Post*, May 23, 2016, https://www.washingtonpost.com/news/monkey-cage/wp/2016/05/23/critics-challenge-our-portrait-of-americas-political-inequality-heres-5-ways-they-are-wrong/?utm_term=.465f2e6e1d3d.

36. Frank Rich, "The Billionaires Bankrolling the Tea Party," *New York Times*, August 28, 2010, https://www.nytimes.com/2010/08/29/opinion/29rich.html.

37. Robert Barnes, "Federalist Society, White House cooperation on judges paying benefits," *Washington Post*, November 18, 2017, https://www.washingtonpost.com/politics/courts_law/federalist-society-white-house-cooperation-on-judges-paying-benefits/2017/11/18/4b69b4da-cb20-11e7-8321-481fd63f174d_story.html.

38. Michelle Ye Hee Lee, "Koch network gears up for the next Supreme Court vacancy," *Washington Post*, January 28, 2018, https://www.washingtonpost.com/news/powerpost/wp/2018/01/28/koch-network-is-gearing-up-for-the-next-supreme-court-vacancy/.

39. https://www.cbsnews.com/news/david-koch-charles-koch-network-is-going-all-in-for-2018-midterms/

40. https://www.washingtonpost.com/politics/trump-to-inherit-more-than-100-court-vacancies-plans-to-reshape-judiciary/2016/12/25/d190dd18-c928-11e6-85b5-76616a33048d_story.html?utm_term=.134288f4f351

41. https://www.commondreams.org/news/2019/02/08/warnings-trumpism-forever-senate-gop-rams-through-44-lifetime-judges-one-day

42. https://www.dailysignal.com/2017/08/10/trump-appoints-more-judges-in-200-days-than-obama-bush-clinton/

43. Eric Lipton, "Scalia Took Dozens of Trips Funded by Private Sponsors, *New York Times*, February 26, 2016, https://www.nytimes.com/2016/02/27/us/politics/scalia-led-court-in-taking-trips-funded-by-private-sponsors.html.

44. Rich Gardella, "Why Don't Supreme Court Justices Have an Ethics Code?" NBC News, April 11, 2017, https://www.nbcnews.com/news/us-news/why-don-t-supreme-court-justices-have-ethics-code-n745236.

45. http://www.hughhewitt.com/senate-majority-leader-mitch-mcconnell-on-the-federal-judiciary-and-the-pace-of-appointments/

46. https://www.youtube.com/watch?v=hDsPWmioSHg
47. https://www.heritage.org/the-constitution/report/commerce-commerce-everywhere-the-uses-and-abuses-the-commerce-clause
48. https://www.thomhartmann.com/users/randy95023/blog/2011/10/iron-heel-capitalism
49. https://www.cnn.com/2019/02/01/world/european-colonization-climate-change-trnd/index.html
50. https://www.theatlantic.com/business/archive/2014/06/slavery-made-america/373288/
51. https://www.measuringworth.com/slavery.php
52. http://www.historynet.com/the-day-new-york-tried-to-secede.htm
53. And this doesn't begin to count the value of the crop that slaves made possible: cotton. The 1860 archive of the *New York Times* contains this article about the cotton trade from the perspective of the British, our principal customers for cotton:

    "Upwards of 500,000 workers are now employed in our cotton factories, and it has been estimated that at least 4,000,000 persons in this country are dependent upon the cotton trade for subsistence. A century ago Lancashire contained a population of only 300,000 persons; it now numbers 2,300,000. In the same period of time this enormous increase exceeds that on any other equal surface of the globe, and is entirely owing to the development of the cotton trade.

    "In 1856 there were in the United Kingdom 2,210 factories, running 28,000,000 spindles and 293,000 looms, by 97,000 horse power. Since that period a considerable number of new mills have been erected and expensive additions have been made to the spinning and weaving machinery of these previously in existence. The amount of actual capital invested in the cotton trade of this kingdom is estimated to be between £60,000,000 and £70,000,000 sterling."

    Along the same lines, the editor of the *New York Evening Post* wrote, "New York belongs almost as much to the South as to the North."
54. Ibid.
55. https://www.timesfreepress.com/news/opinion/freepress/story/2017/aug/20/cooper-there-end-sanitizing/444092/
56. https://www.masshist.org/digitaladams/archive/doc?id=D27
57. https://www.press.uchicago.edu/Misc/Chicago/194876.html
58. https://people.rit.edu/wlrgsh/Prigg_v._Pennsylvania_decision.pdf
59. https://founders.archives.gov/documents/Washington/05-08-02-0244
60. https://harvardlawreview.org/2012/01/is-dred-scott-really-the-worst-opinion-of-all-time-why-prigg-is-worse-than-dred-scott-but-is-likely-to-stay-out-of-the-aeoeanticanonae%C2%9D/

Part Two

1. William E. Leuchtenburg, "When Franklin Roosevelt Clashed with the Supreme Court—and Lost," *Smithsonian*, May 2005, https://www.smithsonianmag.com/history/when-franklin-roosevelt-clashed-with-the-supreme-court-and-lost-78497994/.

2. George S. Grossman, ed., *The Spirit of American Law* (New York: Routledge, 2018), 265–66.

3. https://www.history.com/news/franklin-roosevelt-tried-packing-supreme-court

4. http://www.demog.berkeley.edu/~andrew/1918/figure2.html

5. https://www.smithsonianmag.com/history/when-franklin-roosevelt-clashed-with-the-supreme-court-and-lost-78497994/

6. http://docs.fdrlibrary.marist.edu/030937.html

7. http://www.thomhartmann.com/labor.pdf

8. https://www.senate.gov/artandhistory/history/common/generic/CivilRightsAct1875.htm

9. The bill only gained enough Southern support after any mention of desegregating public school was removed from its text.

10. https://www.law.cornell.edu/supremecourt/text/109/3

11. Ibid.

12. http://law2.umkc.edu/faculty/projects/ftrials/trialheroes/charleshoustonessayf.html

13. http://www.blackpast.org/1849-charles-sumner-equality-law-unconstitutionality-separate-colored-schools-massachusetts

14. https://brownvboard.org/content/opinion-roberts?page=4

15. One great resource for learning more about Houston's life and his role in overturning *Brown* is a documentary called *The Road to Brown*. Another is a website called "Famous Trials," which is run by author and historian Douglas Linder.

16. Genna Rae McNeil, *Groundwork: Charles Hamilton Houston and the Struggle for Civil Rights* (Philadelphia: University of Pennsyvania Press, 1983), 42.

17. Knowingly or not, Muhammad Ali echoed this line in 1967 when he told reporters, "My conscience won't let me go shoot my brother, or some darker people, or some poor hungry people in the mud for big powerful America. And shoot them for what? They never called me nigger, they never lynched me, they didn't put no dogs on me, they didn't rob me of my nationality, rape and kill my mother and father. . . . Shoot them for what? . . . How can I shoot them poor people? Just take me to jail."

18. https://nmaahc.si.edu/blog-post/two-landmark-decisions-fight-equality-and-justice

19. https://www.law.cornell.edu/supremecourt/text/347/483

20. Ibid.

21. Ibid.
22. http://law2.umkc.edu/faculty/projects/ftrials/trialheroes/
    charleshoustonessayf.html
23. https://www.law.cornell.edu/supremecourt/text/362/440
24. Public Papers of the Presidents of the United States: John F.
    Kennedy, August 29, 1962, #655, https://quod.lib.umich.edu/p/
    ppotpus/4730892.1962.001/717?rgn=full+text;view=image.
25. David Brian Robertson and Dennis R., Judd, *The Development of
    American Public Policy: The Structure of Policy Restraint* (Glenview, IL:
    Scott, Foresman/Little, Brown & Co., 1989).
26. Tarla Rei Peterson, ed., *Green Talk in the White House: The Rhetorical
    Presidency Encounters Ecology* (College Station, TX: Texas A&M
    University Press, 2004).
27. Tom Wicker, "Impounding and Implying," *New York Times*, February 8,
    1973.
28. https://caselaw.findlaw.com/us-supreme-court/420/35.html
29. Amanda Little, "A look back at Reagan's environmental record," *Grist*,
    June 11, 2004, https://grist.org/article/griscom-reagan/.
30. https://grist.org/article/epa24/
31. https://www.justice.gov/enrd/massachusetts-v-epa
32. Ibid.
33. https://www.eenews.net/stories/1060087211
34. They included the Council on Environmental Quality, the OMB, the
    Office of Science and Technology Policy, the Department of Energy,
    the Department of the Interior, the Department of Transportation,
    the Department of Agriculture, the Department of Commerce, the
    Department of Defense, and the Department of State (and their various
    department heads).
35. https://docs.justia.com/cases/federal/district-courts/oregon/
    ordce/6:2015cv01517/123110/83
36. https://supreme.justia.com/cases/federal/us/41/367/
37. https://www.ourchildrenstrust.org/
38. *People ex rel. Le Roy v. Hurlbit*, 24 Mich 44, November 29, 1871.
39. https://www.salon.com/2017/09/23/this-is-treason-nixon-vietnam-and-
    the-sordid-story-of-the-chennault-affair/
40. http://prde.upress.virginia.edu/conversations/4006123
41. https://www.csmonitor.com/Commentary/Global-Viewpoint/2013/0305/
    Argo-helps-Iran-s-dictatorship-harms-democracy
42. Ibid.
43. https://www.nytimes.com/1992/10/19/opinion/essay-the-patsy-
    prosecutor.html
44. https://archive.nytimes.com/www.nytimes.com/books/97/06/29/reviews/
    iran-pardon.html?mcubz=0

45. https://www.nytimes.com/1992/08/31/opinion/essay-justice-corrupts-justice.html
46. http://movies2.nytimes.com/learning/general/onthisday/big/1224.html#article
47. https://www.politifact.com/florida/statements/2015/jun/09/hillary-clinton/hillary-clinton-revisits-floridas-2000-and-2004-vo/
48. http://articles.latimes.com/2001/may/21/news/mn-620
49. https://names.mongabay.com/data/black.html
50. https://www.usccr.gov/pubs/vote2000/report/main.htm
51. https://www.youtube.com/watch?v=8GBAsFwPglw
52. https://www.washingtonpost.com/wp-dyn/articles/A31074-2005Jan23.html
53. https://www.nytimes.com/2005/07/28/politics/panel-sends-judge-10page-questionnaire.html
54. Ibid.
55. https://www.washingtonpost.com/archive/opinions/2001/11/16/lessons-of-the-long-recount/6a9967f6-7741-45e3-967c-e07e24474307/
56. http://www.washingtonpost.com/wp-dyn/articles/A12623-2001Nov11_4.html
57. https://www.nytimes.com/2001/11/12/us/examining-vote-overview-study-disputed-florida-ballots-finds-justices-did-not.html
58. While Republican lore with regard to the election of John F. Kennedy in 1960 suggests that Kennedy was also elected by subterfuge or fraud in Chicago, that argument falls apart under analysis. If Chicago—and, indeed, all of Illinois—had voted for Nixon, Kennedy would still have won the election. Paul von Hippel, "Here's a voter fraud myth: Richard Daley 'stole' Illinois for John Kennedy in the 1960 election," *Washington Post*, August 8, 2017, https://www.washingtonpost.com/news/monkey-cage/wp/2017/08/08/heres-a-voter-fraud-myth-richard-daley-stole-illinois-for-john-kennedy-in-the-1960-election/.

Part Three

1. http://teachingamericanhistory.org/library/document/letter-to-john-taylor-2/
2. https://www.nytimes.com/2004/03/18/politics/scalia-angrily-defends-his-duck-hunt-with-cheney.html
3. https://www.huffingtonpost.com/2010/10/20/scalia-thomas-koch-industries_n_769843.html
4. https://en.wikipedia.org/wiki/List_of_overruled_United_States_Supreme_Court_decisions
5. https://en.wikipedia.org/wiki/List_of_abrogated_United_States_Supreme_Court_decisions

6. The list is succinct: The 11th Amendment (1795) overturned the 1793 decision *Chisholm v. Georgia* around the issue of the sovereign immunity of the states; the 13th and 14th Amendments (1865 and 1868) overturned the 1865 *Dred Scott v. Sandford* slavery decision; the 16th Amendment (1913) overturned the Supreme Court's 1895 tax decision in *Pollock v. Farmers' Loan and Trust Co.*; with the 19th Amendment (1920), Congress and the states struck down the 1875 *Minor v. Happersett* decision, which denied women the right to vote; the 26th Amendment (1971) modified the 1970 *Oregon v. Mitchell* decision and gave 18-year-olds the right to vote in federal elections.

7. https://www.equalrightsamendment.org/faq/

8. The leading organizations in this effort are Public Citizen (http://www.publiccitizen.org) and the national Move to Amend coalition (http://www.movetoamend.org).

9. Jonathan Merritt, "Richard Land and Southern Baptists' Race Problem," *Huffington Post*, April 18, 2012, https://www.huffingtonpost.com/jonathan-merritt/richard-land-and-the-southern-baptist-race-problem_b_1430019.html.

10. Nicola Beisel and Tamara Kay, "Abortion, Race, and Gender in Nineteenth-Century America," *American Sociological Review* 69, no. 4 (2004): 498–518, https://journals.sagepub.com/doi/10.1177/000312240406900402.

11. Steven P. Miller, "The evangelical presidency: Reagan's dangerous love affair with the Christian right," *Salon*, May 18, 2014, https://www.salon.com/2014/05/18/the_evangelical_presidency_reagans_dangerous_love_affair_with_the_christian_right/.

12. https://www.archives.gov/files/news/john-roberts/accession-60-88-0498/014-supreme-court-jurisdiction/folder014.pdf

13. Ibid.

14. Bracketed insert contained within Roberts's original memo.

15. https://caselaw.findlaw.com/us-supreme-court/105/381.html

16. https://caselaw.findlaw.com/us-supreme-court/337/582.html

17. https://www.theguardian.com/environment/2017/jul/10/earths-sixth-mass-extinction-event-already-underway-scientists-warn

18. https://www.forbes.com/sites/niallmccarthy/2018/10/12/the-cost-of-climate-related-disasters-soared-in-the-21st-century-infog

ACKNOWLEDGMENTS

Special thanks go to Troy N. Miller, who worked with me for years as a producer and writer for the television show *The Big Picture*, which I hosted every weeknight for seven years in Washington, DC. Troy worked hard as a researcher, sounding board, editor, and often cowriter on parts of this book, and deserves recognition for it.

At Berrett-Koehler Publishers, Steve Piersanti—who's the founder and big cheese there—worked with me to kick off this series. It's been a labor of love for both of us, and I'm so grateful to Steve for his insights, rigor, and passion for this project.

Other people at BK have helped bring this book (and some projects associated with it) to you. They include (alphabetically): María Jesús Aguilo, Charlotte Ashlock, Shabnam Banerjee-McFarland, Valerie Caldwell, Leslie Crandell, Michael Crowley, Sean Davis, James Faani, Matt Fagaly, Sohayla Farman, Maren Fox, Kristen Frantz, Lesley Iura, Kylie Johnston, Arielle Kesweder, Anna Leinberger, Catherine Lengronne, Zoe Mackey, Neal Maillet, David Marshall, Sarah Modlin, Jose Ortega, Courtney Schonfeld, Katie Sheehan, Jeevan Sivasubramaniam (who has helped keep me sane for years), Nina Thompson, Jason VanDenEng, Johanna Vondeling (who edited several of my previous books so brilliantly), Edward Wade, Ginger Winters, Chloe Wong, and Linda Jupiter who did such a great job helping manage the production of this book. BK is an extraordinary publishing company, and it's been an honor to have them publish my books for almost two decades.

They also provided a brilliant final editor for the book, Elissa Rabellino, who did a great job smoothing and tightening the text while also fact-checking.

Former IBEW President Larry Cohen was a tremendous help with the labor issues in this book (which are detailed in a "bonus" PDF on our website), as were labor attorneys Amanda Jaret and Jessica Rutter. Thanks so much!

Bill Gladstone, my agent for over two decades, helped make this book—and the Hidden History series—possible. Bill is truly one of the best in the business.

My executive producer, Shawn Taylor, helped with booking expert guests into our radio and TV programs, many of whom provided great information and anecdotes for this book. And my video producer, Nate Atwell, is a true visual genius. I'm blessed to have such a great team helping me produce a daily radio and TV program, which supports my writing work.

And, as always, my best sounding board, editor, and friend is my wife, Louise. Without her, in all probability none of my books would have ever seen the light of day.

INDEX

ABOUT THE AUTHOR

© Ian Sbalcio

Thom Hartmann is the four-time Project Censored Award–winning, *New York Times* best-selling author of more than 25 books currently in print in over a dozen languages on five continents in the fields of psychiatry, ecology, politics, and economics, and the number one progressive talk show host in the United States.

His daily three-hour radio/TV show is syndicated on commercial radio stations nationwide, on nonprofit and community stations nationwide and in Europe and Africa by Pacifica, across the entire North American continent on SiriusXM Satellite Radio, on its own YouTube channel, via podcast, on Facebook Live, worldwide through the US American Forces Network, and through the Thom Hartmann app in the App Store and for Android. The show is also simulcast as TV in real time into over 60 million US homes by the Free Speech TV network on Dish Network, DirecTV, and cable TV systems nationwide.

He has helped set up hospitals, famine relief programs, schools, and refugee centers in India, Uganda, Australia, Colombia, Russia, Israel, and the United States. Formerly rostered with the state of Vermont as a psychotherapist, founder of the Michigan Healing Arts Center, and licensed as an NLP Trainer by Richard Bandler, he was the originator of the revolutionary Hunter/Farmer Hypothesis to understand attention deficit hyperactivity disorder (ADHD).

In the field of environmentalism, Thom has cowritten and costarred in four documentaries with Leonardo DiCaprio, and is also featured in his documentary theatrical releases *The 11th Hour* and *Ice on Fire*. His book *The Last Hours of Ancient Sunlight*, about the end of the age of oil and the inspiration for *The 11th Hour*, is an international best seller and used as a textbook in many schools.

Thom lives with his wife of 48 years, Louise, and their two dogs and three cats, on the Columbia River in Portland, Oregon. They're the parents of three adult children.

BOOKS BY THOM HARTMANN

Also in the Hidden History series

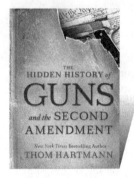

Taking an in-depth, historically informed view, the first book in the Hidden History series examines the brutal role guns have played in American history. Ever practical, Hartmann identifies solutions that can break the power of the gun lobby and put an end to the alarming reality of gun violence in the United States.

Paperback, ISBN 978-1-5230-8599-6
Digital PDF, ISBN 978-1-5230-8600-9
Digital ePub, ISBN 978-1-5230-8601-6
Digital audio, ISBN 978-1-5230-8603-0

In today's America, only a slim majority of registered voters show up for elections. Is this their responsibility alone, or the insidious result of policies made by our elected officials? In the third book in the Hidden History series, Hartmann shows how the war on universal suffrage has been waged for centuries, and is far from over.

Available at bookstores and online on February 4, 2020
Paperback, ISBN 978-1-5230-8778-5
Digital PDF, ISBN 978-1-5230-8779-2
Digital ePub, ISBN 978-1-5230-8780-8
Digital audio, ISBN 978-1-5230-8781-5

Dear reader,

Thank you for picking up this book and welcome to the worldwide BK community! You're joining a special group of people who have come together to create positive change in their lives, organizations, and communities.

What's BK all about?

Our mission is to connect people and ideas to create a world that works for all.

Why? Our communities, organizations, and lives get bogged down by old paradigms of self-interest, exclusion, hierarchy, and privilege. But we believe that can change. That's why we seek the leading experts on these challenges—and share their actionable ideas with you.

A welcome gift

To help you get started, we'd like to offer you a free copy of one of our bestselling ebooks:

www.bkconnection.com/welcome

When you claim your **free ebook,** you'll also be subscribed to our blog.

Our freshest insights

Access the best new tools and ideas for leaders at all levels on our blog at ideas.bkconnection.com.

Sincerely,

Your friends at Berrett-Koehler